GCSE Astronomy
150 Practice Questions on Planets, Asteroids, and Comets
(2022)

Published in Great Britain in 2023

ISBN **9798373531467**

Text and Illustrations Copyright © James Harding

Other books by James Harding

GCSE Astronomy – 150 Practice Questions on the Earth, the Moon, and the Sun (2022)
GCSE Astronomy – 150 Practice Questions on Stars, Galaxies, and the Universe (2022)
GCSE Physics – 200 Practice Questions on Atomic Structure and Radioactivity (2022)
GCSE Chemistry – 150 Practice Questions on Atomic Structure and the Periodic Table (2022)
GCSE Chemistry – 150 Practice Questions on Organic Chemistry (2022)
GCSE Chemistry – 150 Practice Questions on the Chemistry of the Atmosphere and the Environment (2022)
GCSE Physics – 100 Word Searches on Different Topics – For Teachers and Students (2022)
GCSE Chemistry – 100 Word Searches on Different Topics – For Teachers and Students (2022)
GCSE Mathematics – 100 Word Searches on Different Topics – For Teachers and Students (2022)

Did you like this book?

If you liked this book, consider giving it a review where you bought it. This will help others to find the book.

GCSE Astronomy
150 Practice Questions on Planets, Asteroids, and Comets
(2022)

1.) In the heliocentric model of the solar system, what is at the centre?

   i.) Jupiter   ii.) the Moon   (iii.) the Sun   iv.) Mars

[1 mark]

2.) In the geocentric model of the solar system, what is at the centre?

   i.) Jupiter   ii.) the Sun   (iii.) the Earth   iv.) Mars

[1 mark]

3.) In 1610, Italian scientist Galileo Galilei discovered four large objects that appeared to orbit Jupiter. These were the four largest moons of Jupiter: Io, Europa, Ganymede, and Callisto. Explain how this discovery counted as evidence *against* the geocentric model of the solar system.

_____

_____

_____

_____

_____

[2 marks]

4.) In the geocentric model of the solar system, the Earth was thought to be at the centre of the universe, and unmoving. It was thought that, if the Earth *were* moving, the stars would be seen to shift in the night sky – an effect called parallax – and since no parallax was observed, the Earth could not be moving. Nowadays, parallax is observed in stars. Explain why ancient astronomers were not able to see this parallax.

_____

_____

[3 marks]

5.) The diagram below shows the path of Mars across the night sky during 2007-2008. Mars moves in one direction across the night sky, but then reverses direction for a while, before turning back to its original direction. What is this kind of motion called?

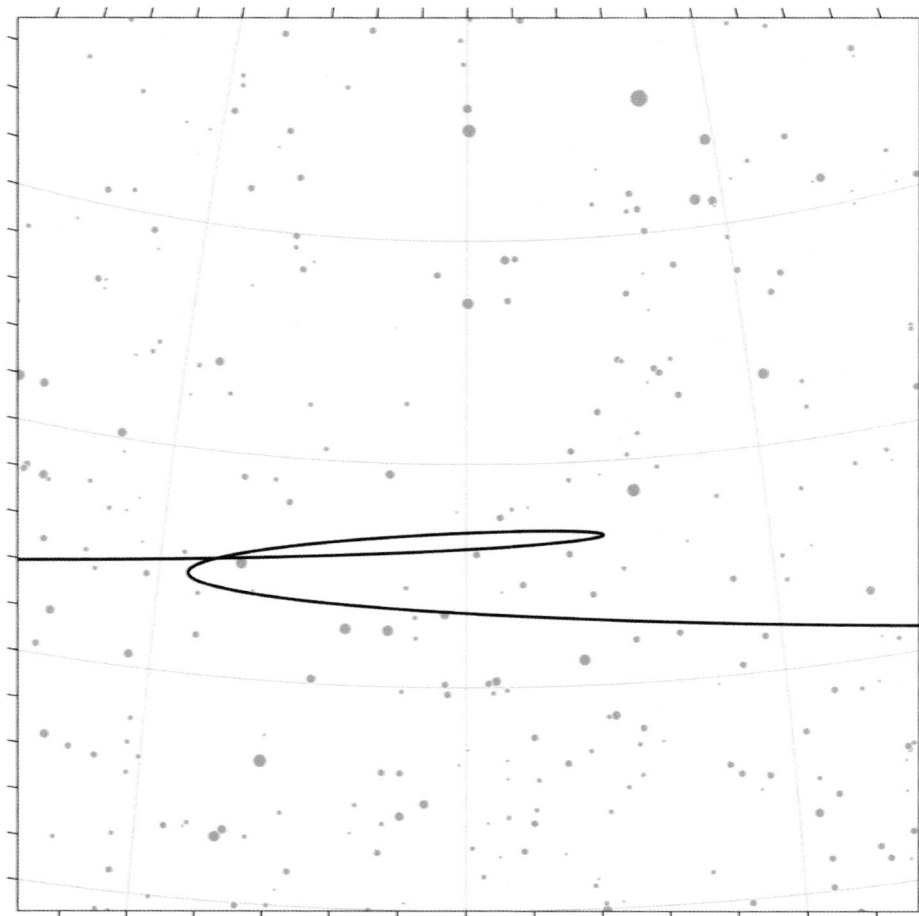

[1 mark]

6.) Give Kepler's First Law.

_____

_____

[3 marks]

7.) The diagram below shows an ellipse. Draw, on the diagram, the **major axis** of the ellipse.

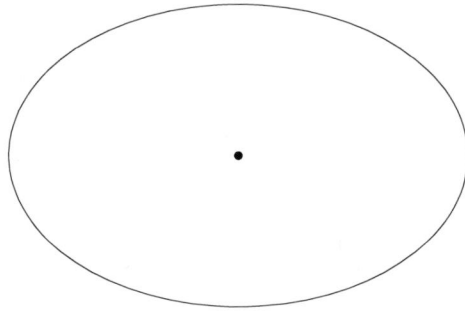

[1 mark]

8.) The diagram below shows an ellipse. Draw, on the diagram, the **minor axis** of the ellipse.

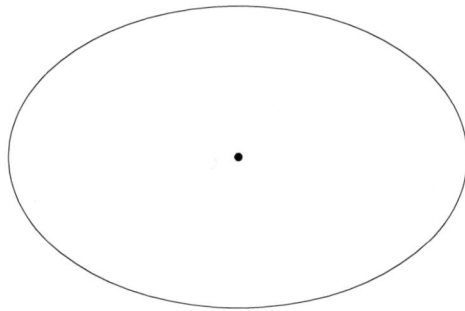

[1 mark]

9.) The diagram below shows an ellipse. Draw, on the diagram, the **semi-minor axis** of the ellipse.

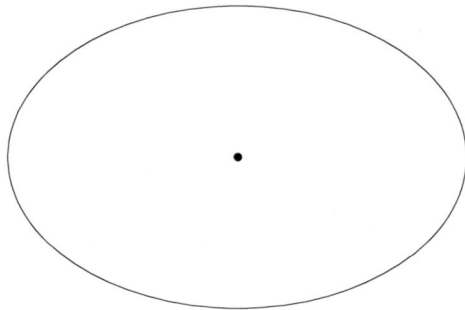

[1 mark]

10.) The diagram below shows an ellipse. Draw, on the diagram, the **semi-major axis** of the ellipse.

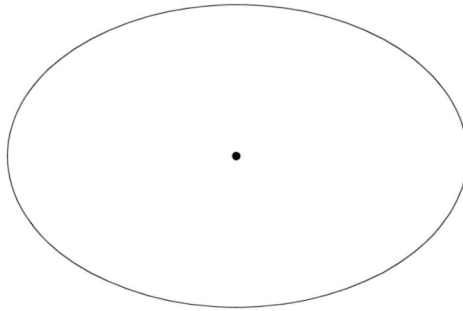

[1 mark]

11.) The diagram below shows an ellipse. The major and minor axes, as well as one focus of the ellipse, are shown. Draw, on the diagram, the location of the **other focus** of the ellipse.

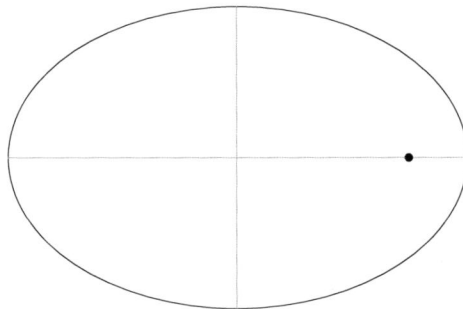

[1 mark]

12.) The diagram below shows an ellipse. The major and minor axes, as well as one focus of the ellipse, are shown. Draw, on the diagram, the location of the **other focus** of the ellipse.

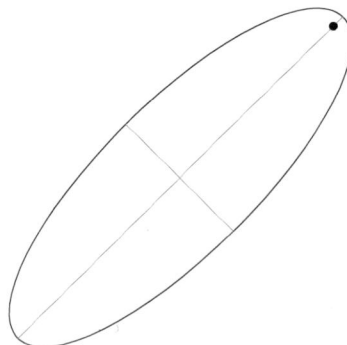

[1 mark]

13.) Below are shown four ellipses.

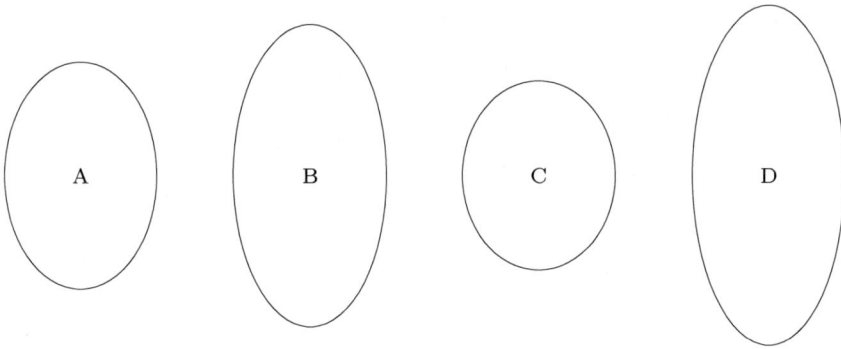

a.) Which ellipse has the **greatest eccentricity**?

_____

[1 mark]

b.) Which ellipse has the **least eccentricity**?

_____

[1 mark]

14.) Below are shown four ellipses.

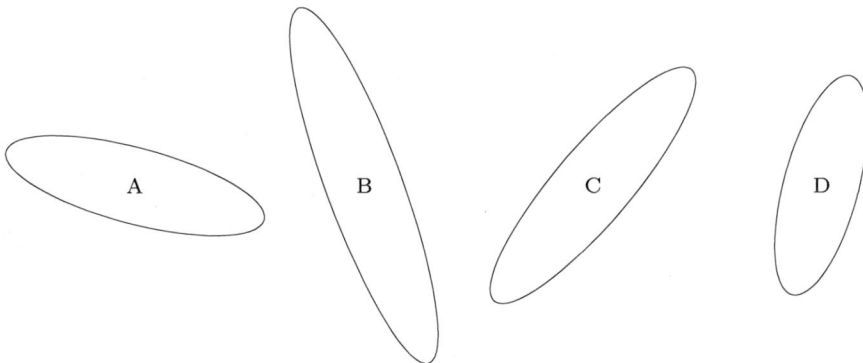

a.) Which ellipse has the **greatest eccentricity**?

_____

[1 mark]

b.) Which ellipse has the **least eccentricity**?

[1 mark]

15.) Below are shown four ellipses, with decreasing eccentricity from left to right. The rightmost ellipse is a circle, which is a special case of an ellipse. Describe the relation between the semi-major and semi-minor axes of an ellipse when it is a circle.

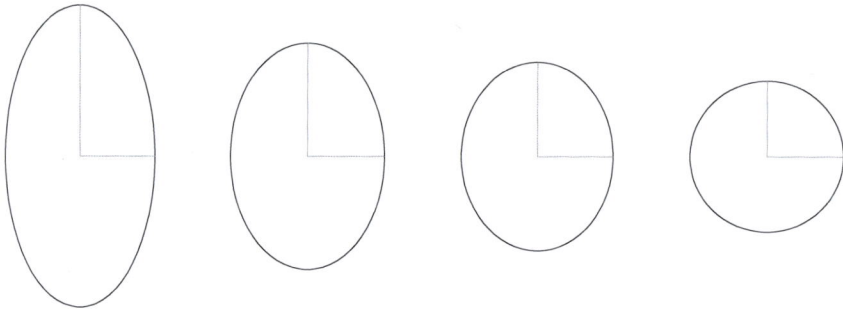

[2 marks]

16.) The diagram below shows the orbit of a comet around the Sun. Mark on the diagram the **aphelion** of the comet's orbit.

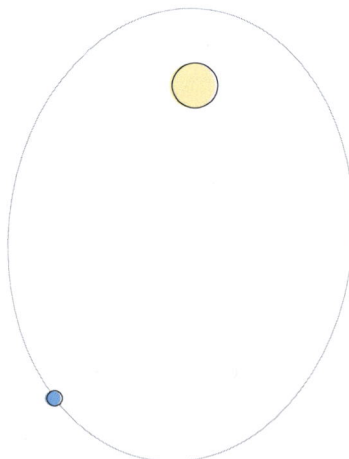

[2 marks]

17.) The diagram below shows the orbit of a comet around the Sun. Mark on the diagram the **perihelion** of the comet's orbit.

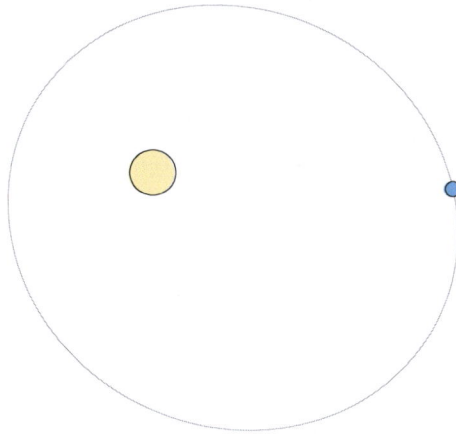

[2 marks]

18.) The diagram below shows the orbit of a comet around the Sun. Mark on the diagram the **perihelion** of the comet's orbit.

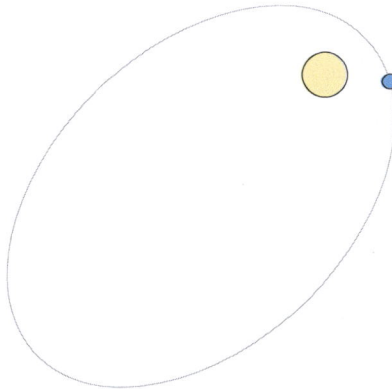

[2 marks]

19.) The diagram below shows the orbit of a comet around the Sun. Mark on the diagram the **aphelion** of the comet's orbit.

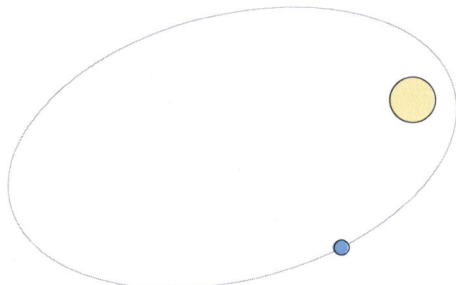

[2 marks]

20.) Give the definition of the term 'perihelion'.

_____

_____

[2 marks]

21.) Give the definition of the term 'aphelion'.

_____

_____

[2 marks]

22.) The diagram below shows the orbit of a satellite around the Earth. Mark on the diagram the **apogee** of the satellite orbit.

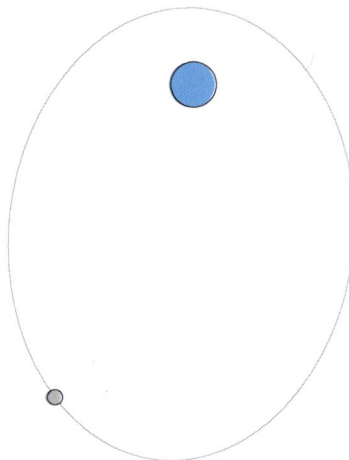

[2 marks]

23.) The diagram below shows the orbit of a satellite around the Earth. Mark on the diagram the **perigee** of the satellite orbit.

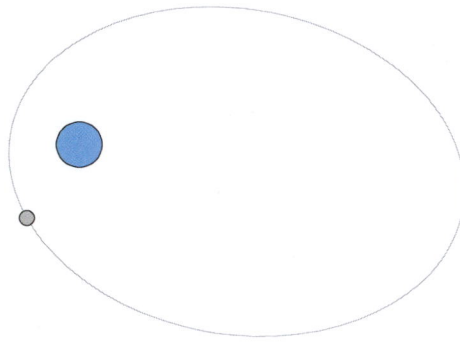

[2 marks]

24.) The diagram below shows the orbit of a satellite around the Earth. Mark on the diagram the **perigee** of the satellite orbit.

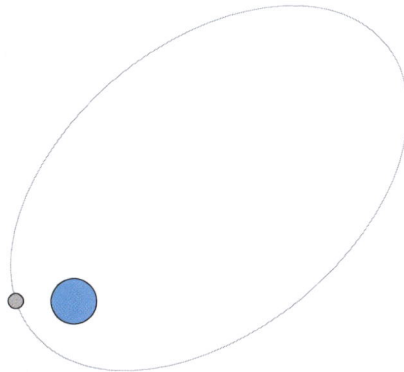

[2 marks]

25.) The diagram below shows the orbit of a satellite around the Earth. Mark on the diagram the **apogee** of the satellite orbit.

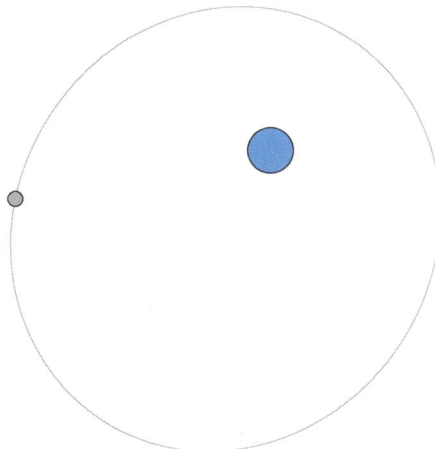

[2 marks]

26.) Give the definition of the term 'apogee'.

_____

_____

[2 marks]

27.) Give the definition of the term 'perigee'.

_____

_____

[2 marks]

28.) The diagram below shows a comet in orbit around the Sun. Draw an arrow on the diagram showing the direction of the gravitational force acting on the comet at this point in its orbit.

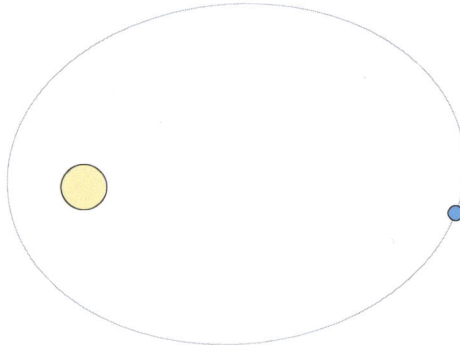

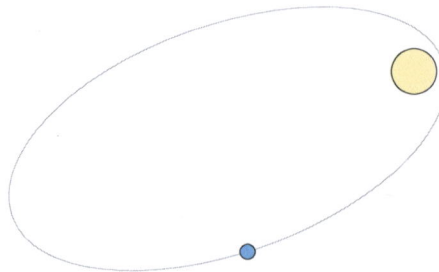

[2 marks]

29.) The diagram below shows a comet in orbit around the Sun. Draw an arrow on the diagram showing the direction of the gravitational force acting on the comet at this point in its orbit.

[2 marks]

30.) The diagram below shows a comet in orbit around the Sun. Draw an arrow on the diagram showing the direction of the instantaneous velocity of the comet at this point in its orbit. Assume that the comet is orbiting clockwise.

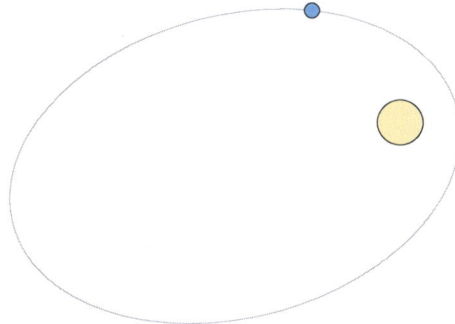

[2 marks]

31.) The diagram below shows a comet in orbit around the Sun. Draw an arrow on the diagram showing the direction of the instantaneous velocity of the comet at this point in its orbit. Assume that the comet is orbiting clockwise.

[2 marks]

32.) Give Kepler's Second Law.

_____

_____

_____

[3 marks]

33.) Which of the following formulae shows the relation between the period of a planet's orbit, T, and the semi-major axis of its orbit, a, in Kepler's Third Law?

   i.) $\frac{T^2}{a^3} = $ constant

   ii.) $\frac{T^2}{a} = $ constant

   iii.) $\frac{T}{a^3} = $ constant

   iv.) $\frac{T^3}{a^3} = $ constant

[1 mark]

34.) Which of the following formulae shows the relation between the periods, T_1 and T_2, and semi-major axes, a_1 and a_2, of the orbits of two planets in the same star system?

   i.) $\frac{T_1^2}{a_1^3} = \frac{T_2^2}{a_2^3}$

   ii.) $\frac{T_1^2}{a_2^3} = \frac{a_1^3}{T_2^2}$

   iii.) $\frac{T_1^2}{a_1^3} = \frac{a_2^3}{T_2^2}$

   iv.) $\frac{T_1^2}{a_1^3} = \frac{T_2^3}{a_2^2}$

[2 marks]

35.) Kepler's Third Law can be written as $\frac{T^2}{a^3} = $ constant, where T is the period of a planet's orbit, and a is the semi-major axis of the planet's orbit. Which of the following is the constant of this equation dependent on?

   i.) the average density of the star

   ii.) the mass of the host star

   iii.) the temperature of the host star

   iv.) the average density of the planet

[1 mark]

36.) Earth has an orbital period of 365.25 dy and an orbital semi-major axis of 1 AU. Use these values and Kepler's Third Law to find the orbital semi-major axis of Jupiter, which has an orbital period of 4330 dy. Give your answer in AU to 3 significant figures.

[3 marks]

37.) Earth has an orbital period of 365.25 dy and an orbital semi-major axis of 1 AU. Use these values and Kepler's Third Law to find the orbital semi-major axis of Uranus, which has an orbital period of 30700 dy. Give your answer in AU to 3 significant figures.

_____

[3 marks]

38.) A scientist predicts that there is a ninth planet very far out in the solar system, with an orbital semi-major axis of 161 AU. Use Kepler's Third Law, as well as the orbital period and semi-major axis of the Earth, to work out the period of this ninth planet's orbit. Give your answer in years to 3 significant figures.

_____

[4 marks]

39.) Which of the following statements is true?

i.) The gravitational force between two objects is **proportional** to the **product** of the masses of the two objects.

ii.) The gravitational force between two objects is **inversely proportional** to the **difference** in the masses of the two objects.

iii.) The gravitational force between two objects is **proportional** to the **sum** of the masses of the two objects.

[1 mark]

40.) Which of the following statements is true?

i.) The gravitational force between two objects is **proportional** to the distance between the centres of mass of the objects.

ii.) The gravitational force between two objects is **inversely proportional** to the distance between the centres of mass of the objects **squared**.

iii.) The gravitational force between two objects is **proportional** to the distance between the centres of mass of the objects **squared**.

[1 mark]

41.) Which of the following is a **superior** planet to Earth?

i.) Mercury   ii.) Venus   iii.) Mars

[1 mark]

42.) Which of the following is a **superior** planet to Earth?

i.) Mercury   ii.) Jupiter   iii.) Venus

[1 mark]

43.) Which of the following is an **inferior** planet to Earth?

i.) Venus   ii.) Jupiter   iii.) Uranus   iv.) Mars

[1 mark]

44.) Which of the following is an **inferior** planet to Saturn?

i.) Uranus   ii.) Neptune   iii.) Mercury

[1 mark]

45.) Which of the following is a **superior** planet to Saturn?

i.) Uranus   ii.) Mars   iii.) Earth   iv.) Jupiter

[1 mark]

46.) How many **inferior planets to Earth** are there?

i.) 6   ii.) 5   iii.) 7   iv.) 2

[1 mark]

47.) How many **inferior planets to Jupiter** are there?

i.) 4   ii.) 2   iii.) 5   iv.) 7

[1 mark]

48.) How many **superior planets to Earth** are there?

i.) 1   ii.) 5   iii.) 3   iv.) 4

[1 mark]

49.) How many **superior planets to Saturn** are there?

i.) 2   ii.) 6   iii.) 4   iv.) 1

[1 mark]

50.) For which planet of the solar system are there **no** inferior planets?

i.) Mercury   ii.) Venus   iii.) Earth   iv.) Saturn

[1 mark]

51.) For which planet of the solar system are there **no** superior planets?

i.) Neptune   ii.) Venus   iii.) Earth   iv.) Uranus

[1 mark]

52.) The diagram below shows the planets of the solar system. The relative sizes and orbital radii of the planets have been exaggerated for clarity.

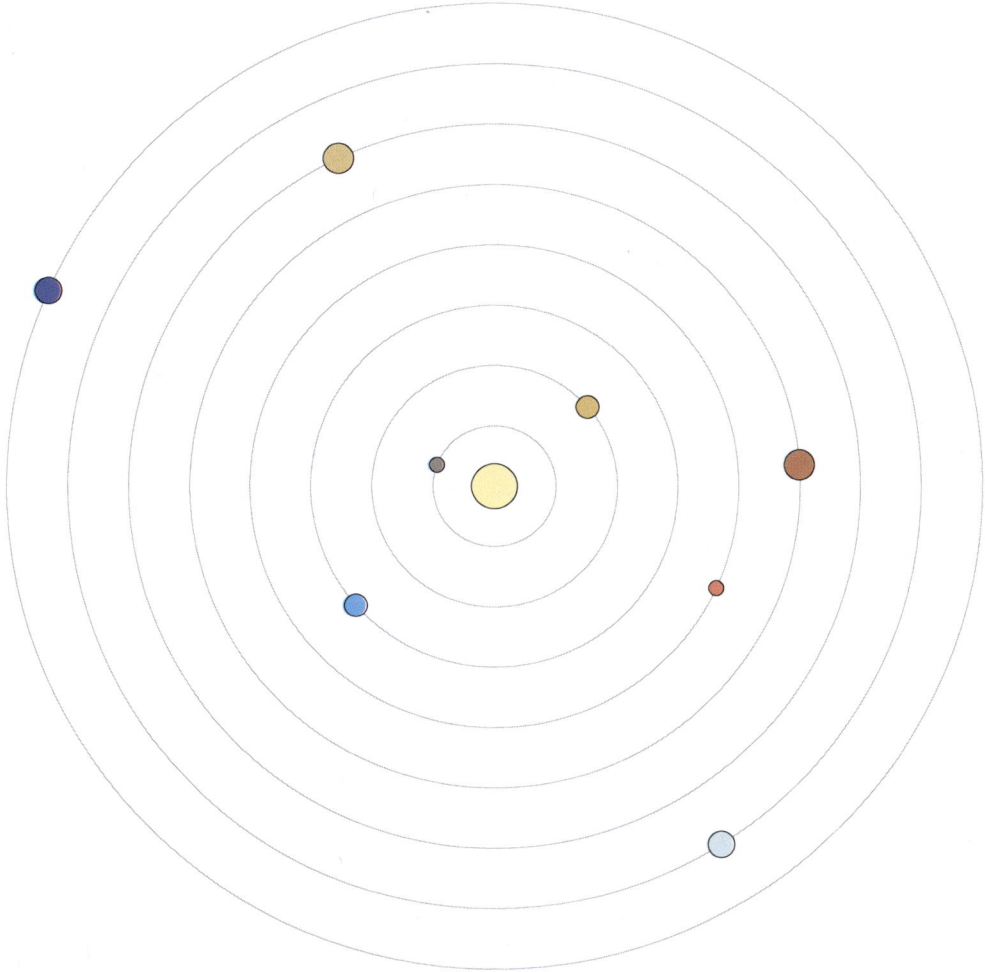

Which planet is in **superior conjunction** with Earth?

i.) Venus   ii.) Jupiter   iii.) Neptune   iv.) Saturn

[1 mark]

53.) The diagram below shows the planets of the solar system. The relative sizes and orbital radii of the planets have been exaggerated for clarity.

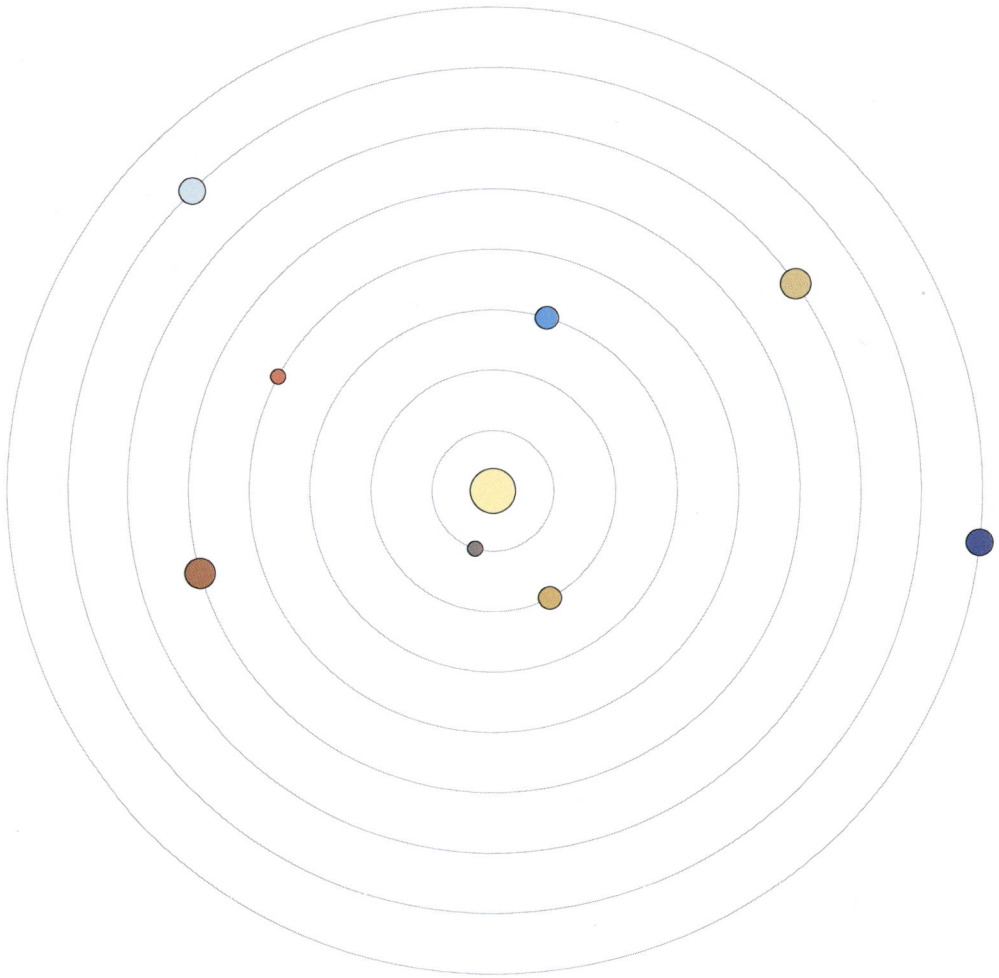

Which planet is in **superior conjunction** with Earth?

   i.) Jupiter   ii.) Mercury   iii.) Venus   iv.) Neptune

[1 mark]

54.) The diagram below shows the planets of the solar system. The relative sizes and orbital radii of the planets have been exaggerated for clarity.

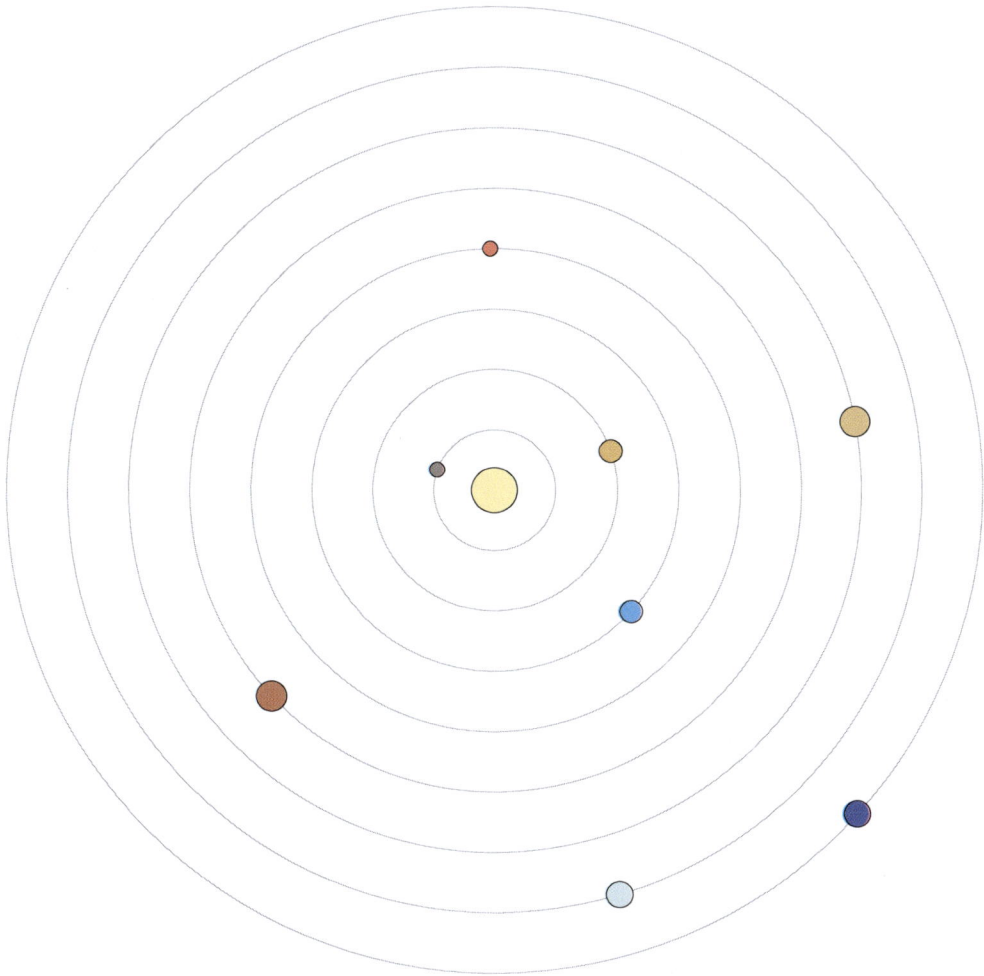

Which planet is in **opposition** with Earth?

i.) Mercury   ii.) Jupiter   iii.) Saturn   iv.) Neptune

[1 mark]

55.) The diagram below shows the planets of the solar system. The relative sizes and orbital radii of the planets have been exaggerated for clarity.

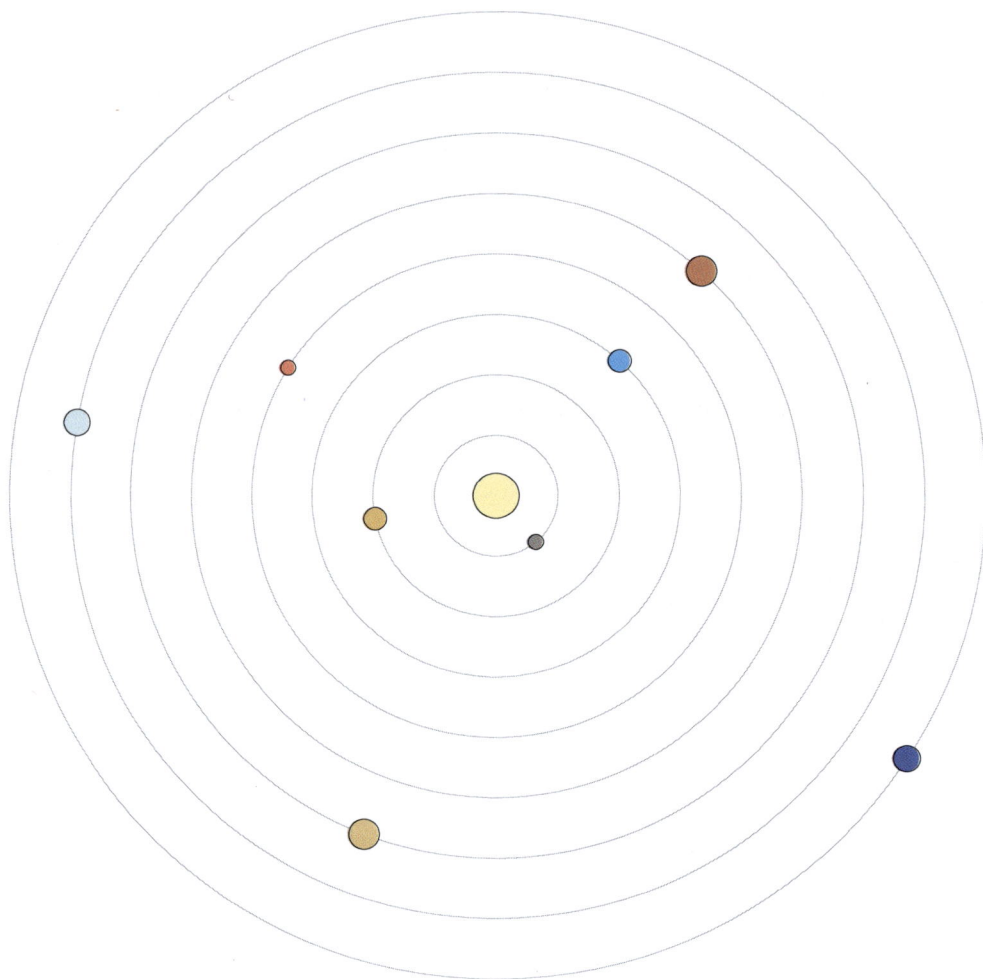

Which planet is in **opposition** with Earth?

  i.) Jupiter   ii.) Mercury   iii.) Neptune   iv.) Uranus

[1 mark]

56.) The diagram below shows the planets of the solar system. The relative sizes and orbital radii of the planets have been exaggerated for clarity.

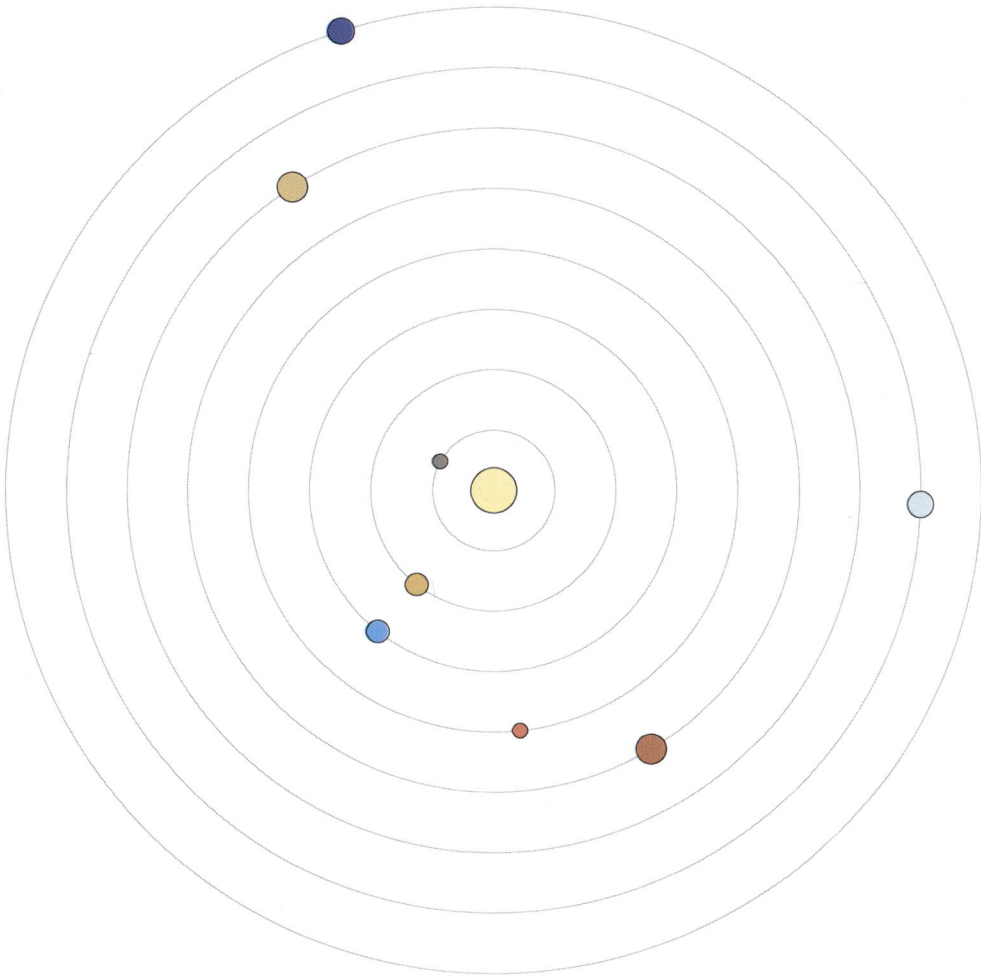

Which planet is in **inferior conjunction** with Earth?

i.) Venus   ii.) Mercury   iii.) Mars   iv.) Uranus

[1 mark]

57.) The diagram below shows the planets of the solar system. The relative sizes and orbital radii of the planets have been exaggerated for clarity.

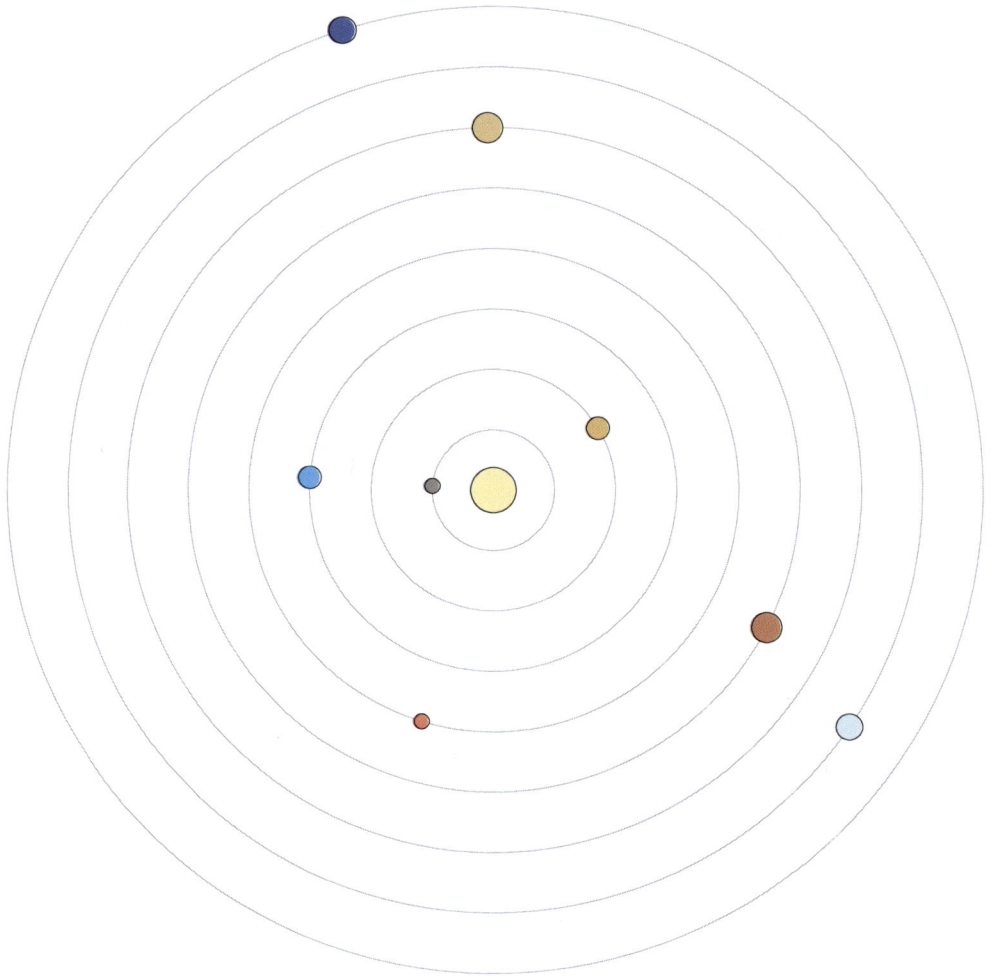

Which planet is in **inferior conjunction** with Earth?

i.) Mercury   ii.) Jupiter   iii.) Venus   iv.) Neptune

[1 mark]

58.) The diagram below shows the planets of the solar system. The relative sizes and orbital radii of the planets have been exaggerated for clarity.

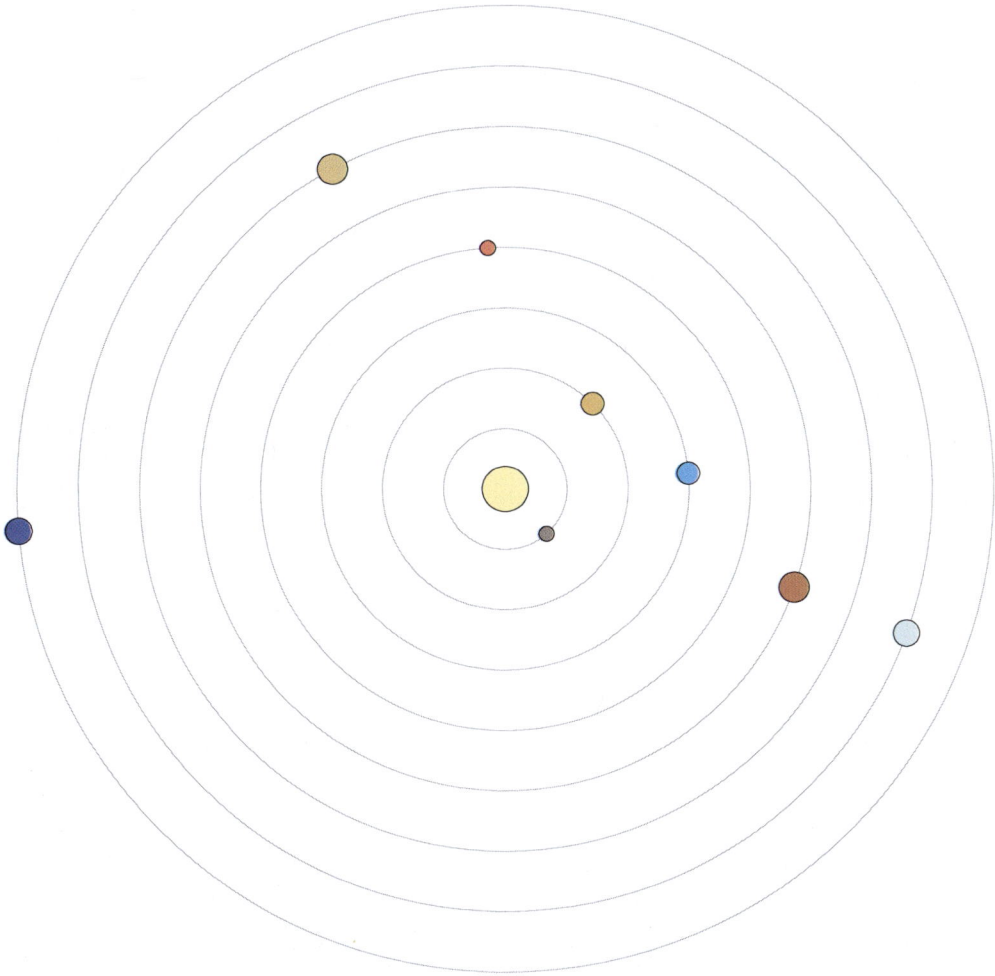

Which planet is in **conjunction** with Earth?

i.) Uranus   ii.) Saturn   iii.) Neptune   iv.) Jupiter

[1 mark]

59.) The diagram below shows the planets of the solar system. The relative sizes and orbital radii of the planets have been exaggerated for clarity.

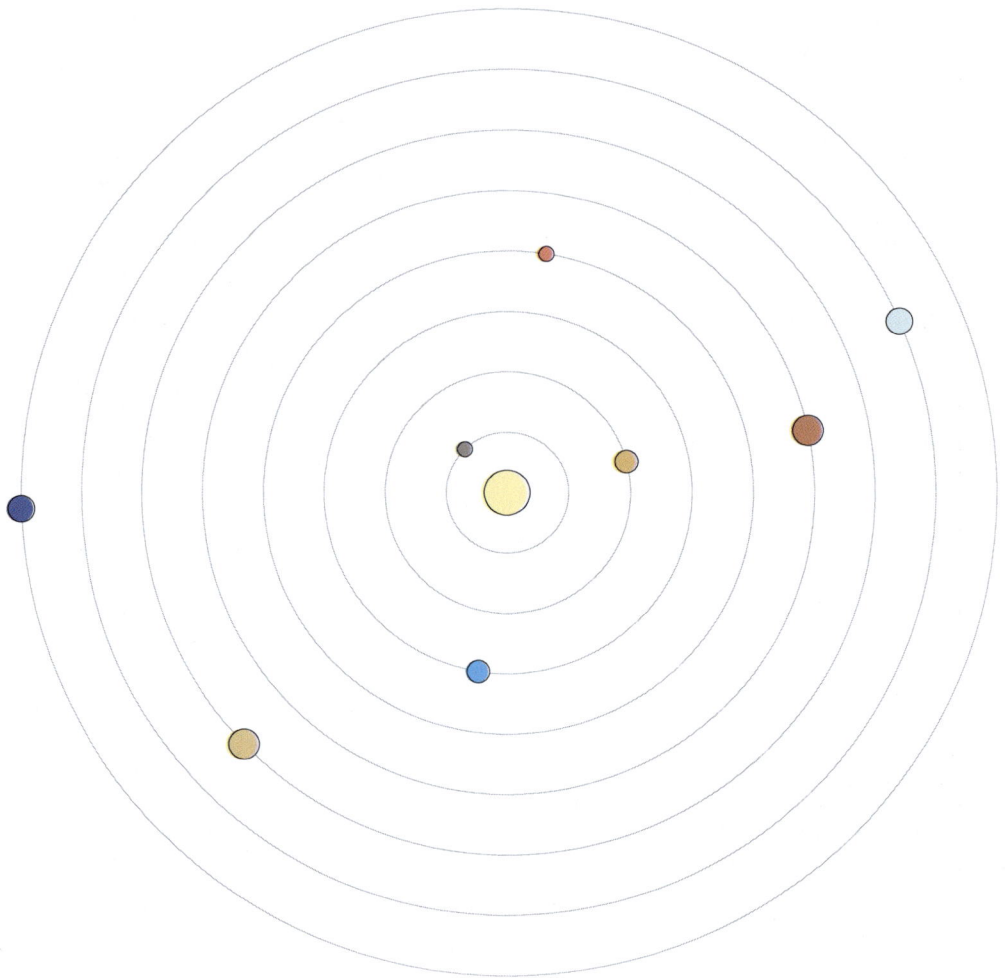

Which planet is in **conjunction** with Earth?

   i.) Saturn   ii.) Mercury   iii.) Mars   iv.) Venus

[1 mark]

60.) Do the planets of the solar system orbit **clockwise** or **anticlockwise** when the solar system is viewed from above?

   i.) clockwise   ii.) anticlockwise

[1 mark]

61.) The diagram below shows the orbits of Venus and Earth around the Sun. At which of the positions A, B, C, or D is Venus at its **greatest elongation** to Earth?

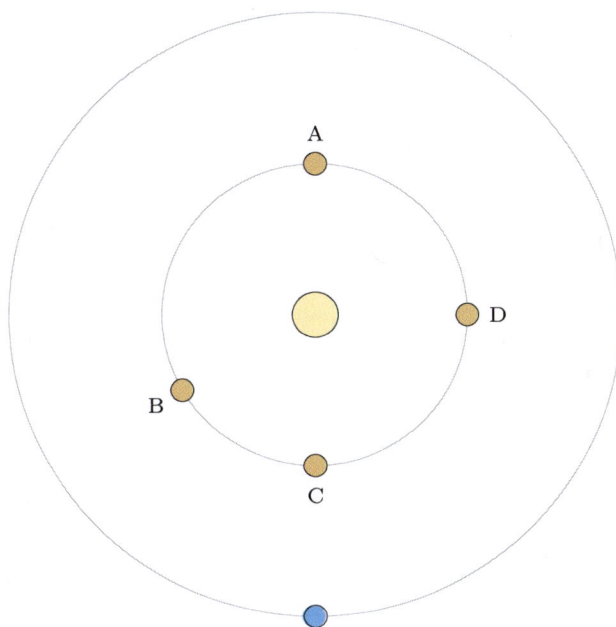

[1 mark]

62.) The diagram below shows Mercury and Earth in their orbits around the Sun. Mercury is at its greatest elongation to Earth, and the Sun-Mercury-Earth system forms a right-angled triangle. Use trigonometry to find the **angle of elongation**. Use a value of $0.387\,\text{AU}$ for the distance between the Sun and Mercury, and a value of $1\,\text{AU}$ for the distance between the Sun and Earth. Give your answer to 1 decimal place.

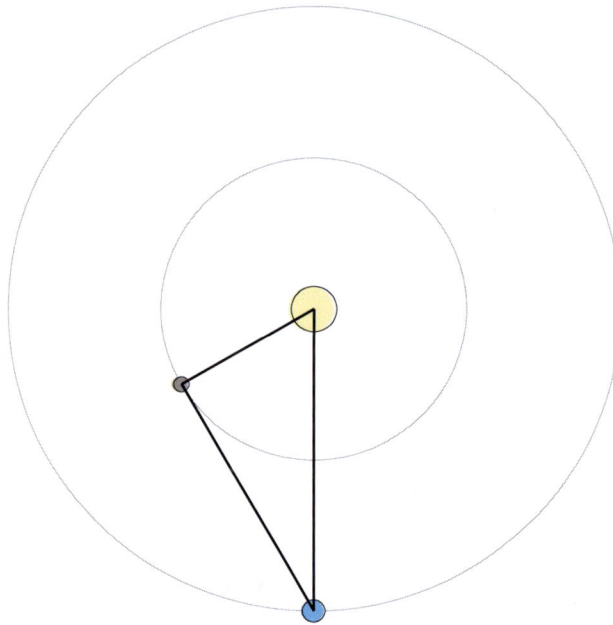

[4 marks]

63.) What is the **ecliptic**?

_____

_____

_____

[3 marks]

64.) a.) Each of the planets of the solar system has an adjectival form of its name. Sometimes these adjectival forms are a bit unusual, and sometimes there are more than one. Which of the following are the correct adjectival forms of 'Mercury'?

    i.) Mercurine   ii.) Mercurial   iii.) Mercurian   iv.) Mercurite

[1 mark]

b.) Which of the following are the correct adjectival forms of 'Venus'?

    i.) Venusian   iii.) Cytherean   v.) Venician

    ii.) Venerian   iv.) Venetian   vi.) Venerean

[1 mark]

c.) Which of the following are the correct adjectival forms of 'Earth'?

i.) Tellurite   iii.) Terran   v.) Earthian

ii.) Terrestrial   iv.) Tellurian   vi.) Territe

[1 mark]

d.) Which of the following are the correct adjectival forms of 'Mars'?

i.) Marsian   ii.) Martian   iii.) Martial   iv.) Marsean

[1 mark]

e.) Which of the following are the correct adjectival forms of 'Jupiter'?

i.) Jupiterian   ii.) Jovial   iii.) Jupiterial   iv.) Jovian

[1 mark]

f.) Which of the following are the correct adjectival forms of 'Saturnian'?

i.) Kronian   ii.) Saturnial   iii.) Cronian   iv.) Saturnian

[1 mark]

g.) Which of the following are the correct adjectival forms of 'Uranus'?

i.) Urinal   ii.) Uranium   iii.) Uranian   iv.) Uranial

[1 mark]

h.) Which of the following are the correct adjectival forms of 'Neptune'?

i.) Neptunian   ii.) Poseidean   iii.) Neptunial   iv.) Neptunean

[1 mark]

65.) Below is a photograph of Jupiter, taken by the Hubble Space Telescope in 2014.

Credit: NASA, ESA, and A. Simon (Goddard Space Flight Center) [1]

a.) What **type** of planet is Jupiter?

   i.) a sub-Earth   iii.) a gas giant

   ii.) a super-Earth   iv.) an ice giant

[1 mark]

b.) Compare the **size** of Jupiter to the other planets in the solar system.

_____

_____

[2 marks]

c.) Jupiter's atmosphere is about $3000\,\mathrm{km}$ deep. What element makes up 90% of Jupiter's atmosphere by volume?

i.) hydrogen   ii.) neon   iii.) helium   iv.) nitrogen

[1 mark]

d.) Jupiter has a mass of $1.9 \times 10^{27}\,\text{kg}$ and a volume of $1.43 \times 10^{24}\,\text{m}^3$. Calculate the **average density** of Jupiter. Give your answer in units of kg/m^3 to 3 significant figures.

_____

[2 marks]

e.) Is the **average density** of Jupiter less than or greater than the **average density** of Earth? Use the internet to look up the average density of the Earth.

  i.) The average density of Jupiter is **less than** the average density of Earth.

  ii.) The average density of Jupiter is **greater than** the average density of Earth.

[2 marks]

66.) Below is a photograph of Saturn, taken by the Cassini space probe in 2007. The exposure is very high, to make the rings of Saturn as visible as possible.

Credit: NASA [2]

What are the rings of Saturn made of?

_____

_____

[2 marks]

67.) What is the **asteroid belt**?

_____

_____

_____

[3 marks]

68.) What is the **Kuiper Belt**?

_____

_____

_____

_____

_____

[4 marks]

69.) What is the **Oort Cloud**?

_____

_____

_____

_____

_____

[4 marks]

70.) What is the **heliosphere**?

_____

_____

_____

[3 marks]

71.) What is the **heliopause**?

_____

_____

[2 marks]

72.) Below is a photo of the dwarf planet Ceres. Describe the location of Ceres in the solar system.

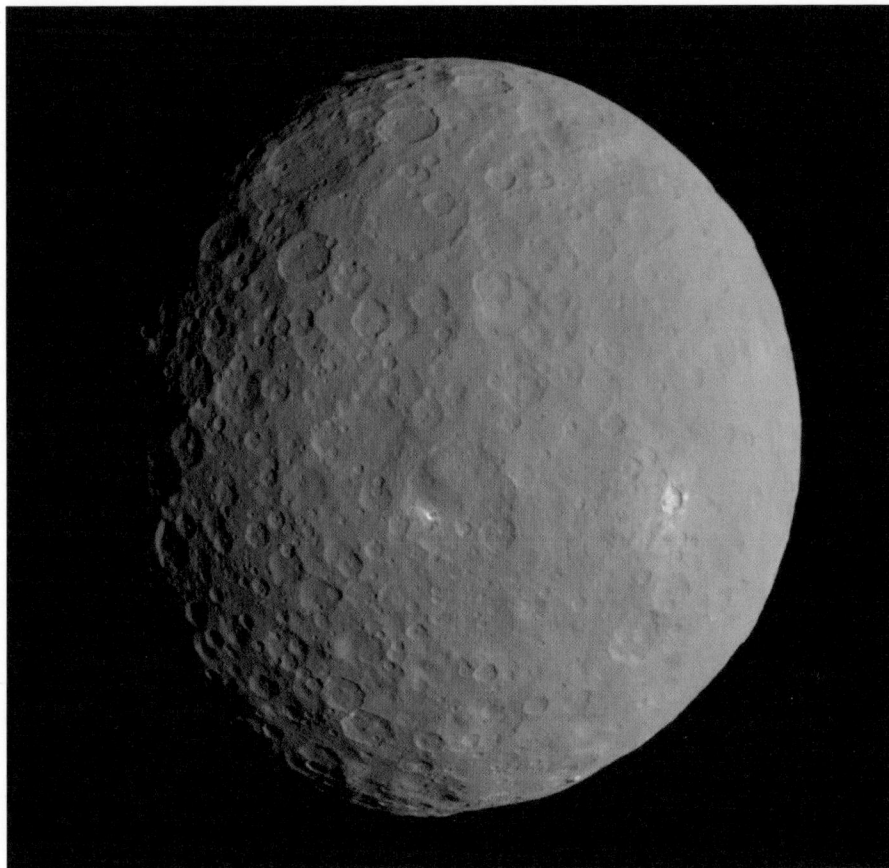

Credit: NASA / JPL-Caltech / UCLA / MPS / DLR / IDA / Justin Cowart [3]

_____

_____

[2 marks]

73.) Below is a photo of the dwarf planet Makemake taken by the Hubble Space Telescope. Describe the location of Makemake in the solar system.

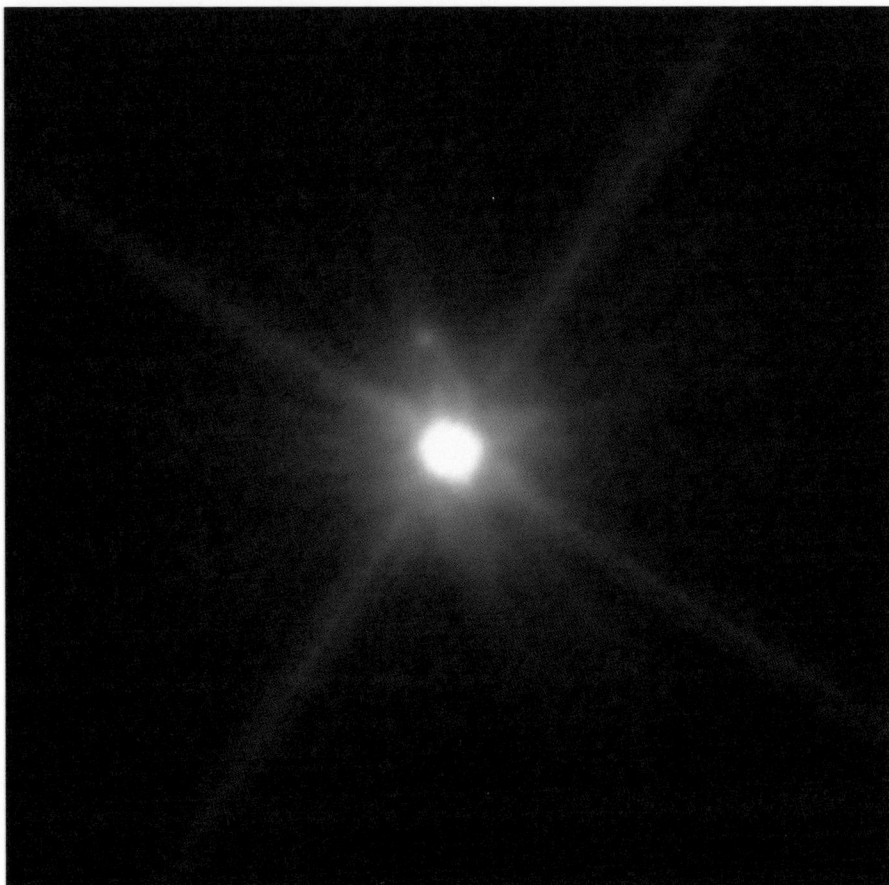

Credit: NASA, ESA, and A. Parker and M. Buie (Southwest Research Institute) [4]

_____

_____

[2 marks]

74.) Below is a photo of Pluto taken by the New Horizons spacecraft in 2015. Before 2006, Pluto was considered to be a planet, but is now considered to be a dwarf planet. Explain why.

Credit: NASA / Johns Hopkins University Applied Physics Laboratory / Southwest Research Institute / Alex Parker

[5]

_____

_____

_____

[2 marks]

75.) What type of object is shown in the photograph below?

Credit: NASA / Dan Burbank [6]

[1 mark]

76.) Which of the following statements is true?

i.) Comets typically have orbits with **high eccentricities**.

ii.) Comets typically have orbits with **low eccentricities**.

[1 mark]

77.) Describe the **chemical composition** of comet nuclei.

[5 marks]

78.) What is the **coma** of a comet?

[3 marks]

79.) Comets typically produce two 'tails' when they are near to the Sun – an **ion tail** and a **dust tail**. One of these tails points directly away from the Sun in a straight line, and the other forms a curve away from the Sun. Which is which, and why?

[3 marks]

80.) What is 'dust' in the context of astronomy?

[4 marks]

81.) Halley's Comet is the only known comet to regularly be visible to the naked eye from Earth. It's visible from Earth every 75 to 79 years. Is Halley's Comet a **short period** comet or a **long period** comet?

i.) a short period comet   ii.) a long period comet

[1 mark]

82.) Churyumov-Gerasimenko is a comet that was visited by the Rosetta spacecraft in 2016. It has an orbital period of 6.4 years. Is Churyumov-Gerasimenko a **short period** comet or a **long period** comet?

i.) a short period comet   ii.) a long period comet

[1 mark]

83.) Below is a photograph of the asteroid Vesta. Vesta is one of the largest asteroids in the solar system, and is at a distance of about 2.36 AU from the Sun. Which group of asteroids is Vesta in?

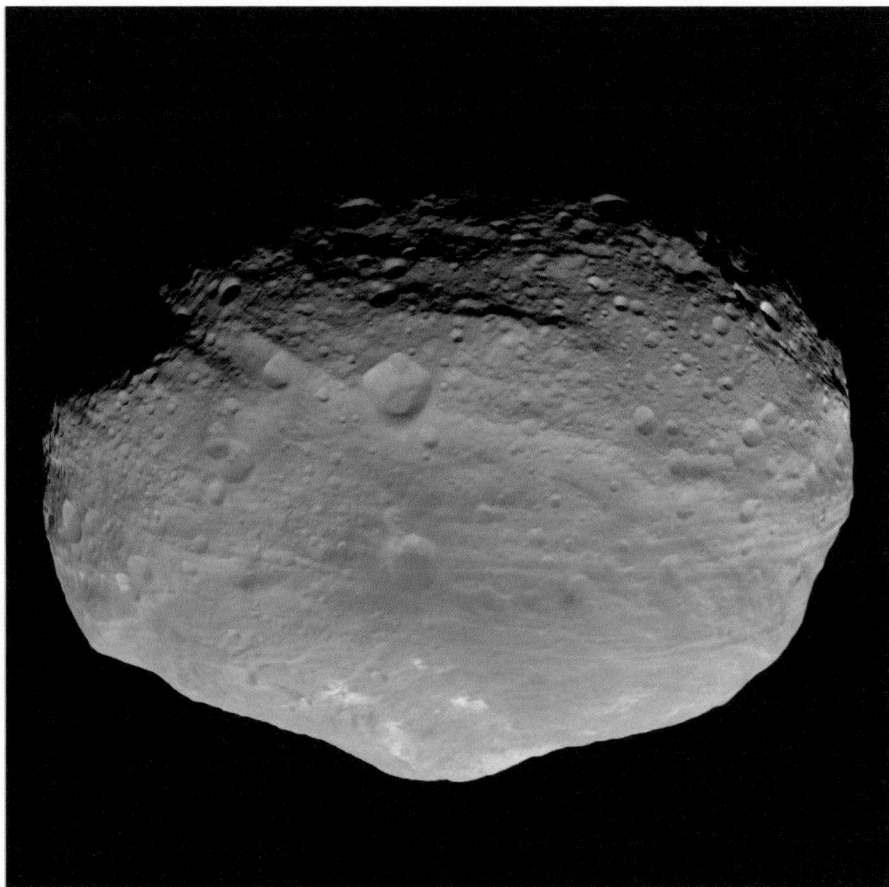

Credit: NASA / JPL / MPS / DLR / IDA / Björn Jónsson [7]

[1 mark]

84.) Describe the typical **chemical composition** of asteroids.

[5 marks]

85.) What are **meteors**?

[3 marks]

86.) What are **meteorites**?

[2 marks]

87.) What are **meteoroids**?

[3 marks]

88.) What is a **refracting telescope**?

[2 marks]

89.) What type of lens is shown in the diagram below?

    i.) a convex lens   ii.) a concave lens

[1 mark]

90.) What type of lens is shown in the diagram below?

    i.) a concave lens   ii.) a convex lens

[1 mark]

91.) The diagram below shows parallel rays passing into a convex lens. On the far side of the lens, are the rays **converging** or **diverging**?

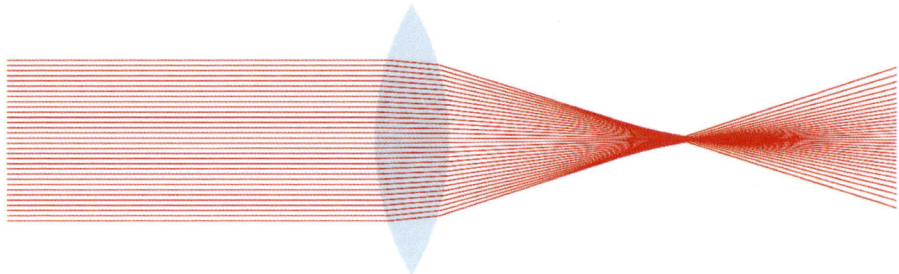

    i.) diverging   ii.) converging

[1 mark]

92.) The diagram below shows parallel rays passing into a concave lens. On the far side of the lens, are the rays **converging** or **diverging**?

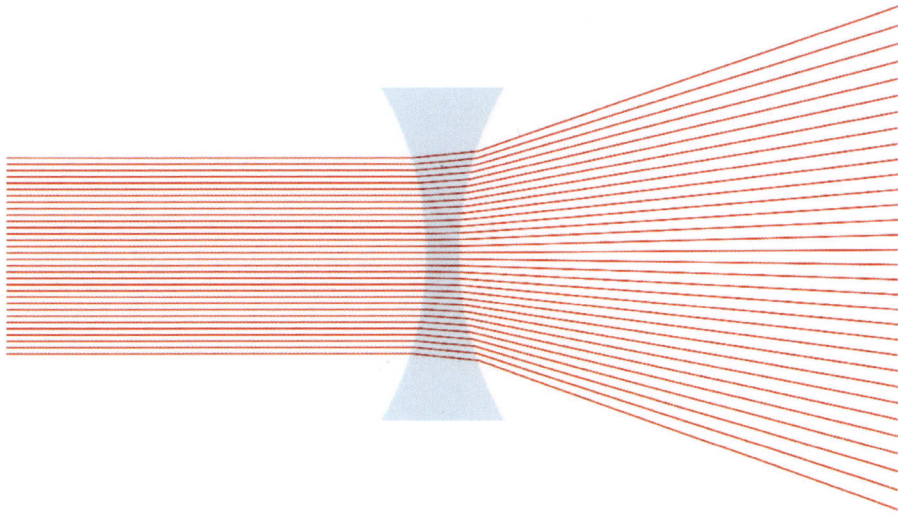

i.) converging

ii.) diverging

[1 mark]

93.) The diagram below represents a type of **ideal lens**. Does it represent a **convex ideal lens** or a **concave ideal lens**?

i.) a concave ideal lens

ii.) a convex ideal lens

[1 mark]

94.) The diagram below represents a type of **ideal lens**. Does it represent a **convex ideal lens** or a **concave ideal lens**?

i.) a concave ideal lens   ii.) a convex ideal lens

[1 mark]

95.) The diagram below shows parallel rays passing into a real convex lens and parallel rays passing into an ideal convex lens. Describe the differences between how the real lens and the ideal lens affect the light rays.

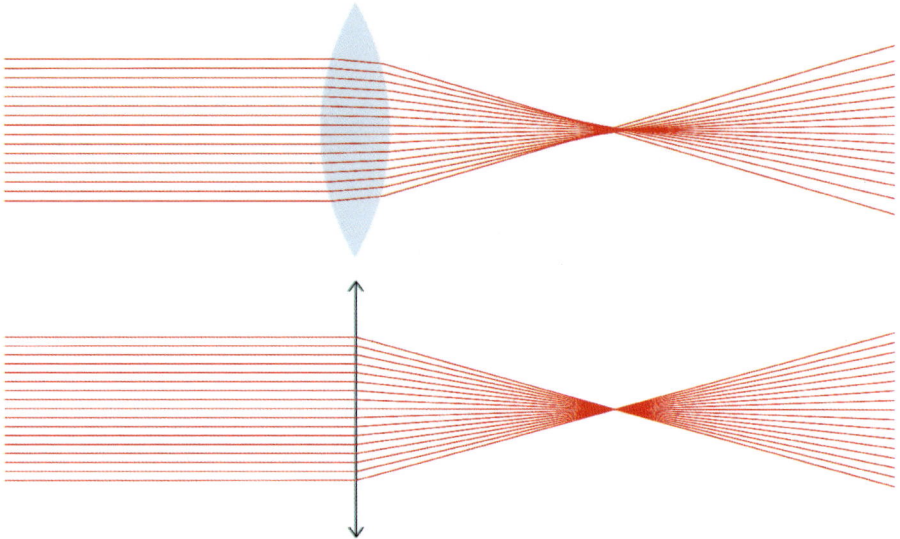

_____

_____

_____

_____

_____

[4 marks]

96.) The diagram below shows parallel rays incident on a curved mirror. Is the mirror a **convex mirror** or a **concave mirror**?

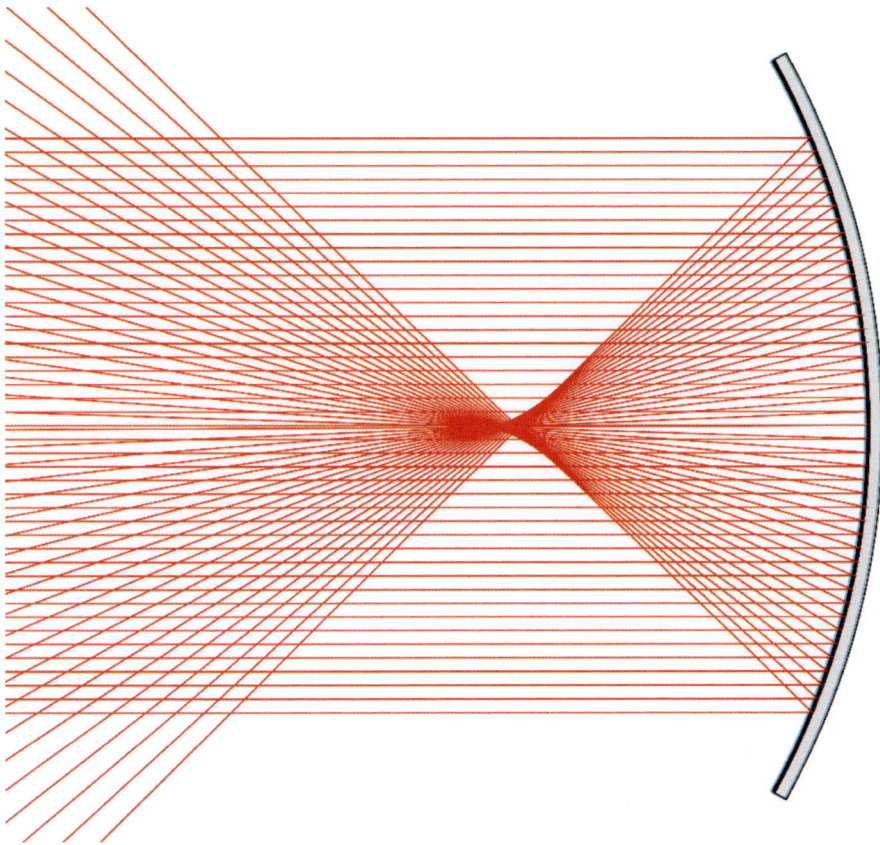

i.) a concave mirror   ii.) a convex mirror

[1 mark]

97.) The diagram below shows parallel rays incident on a curved mirror. Is the mirror a **convex mirror** or a **concave mirror**?

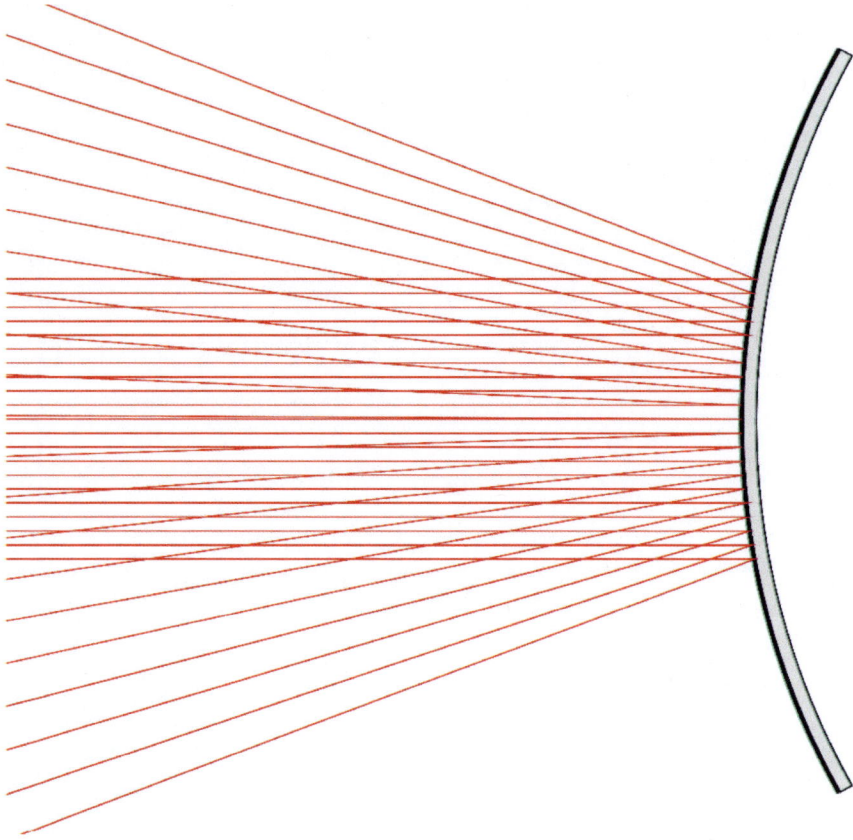

i.) a concave mirror   ii.) a convex mirror

[1 mark]

98.) The diagram below shows parallel rays of light incident on a concave **spherical** mirror. For a spherical mirror, every point on the surface of the mirror is the same distance away from a single point, called the **centre of curvature**.

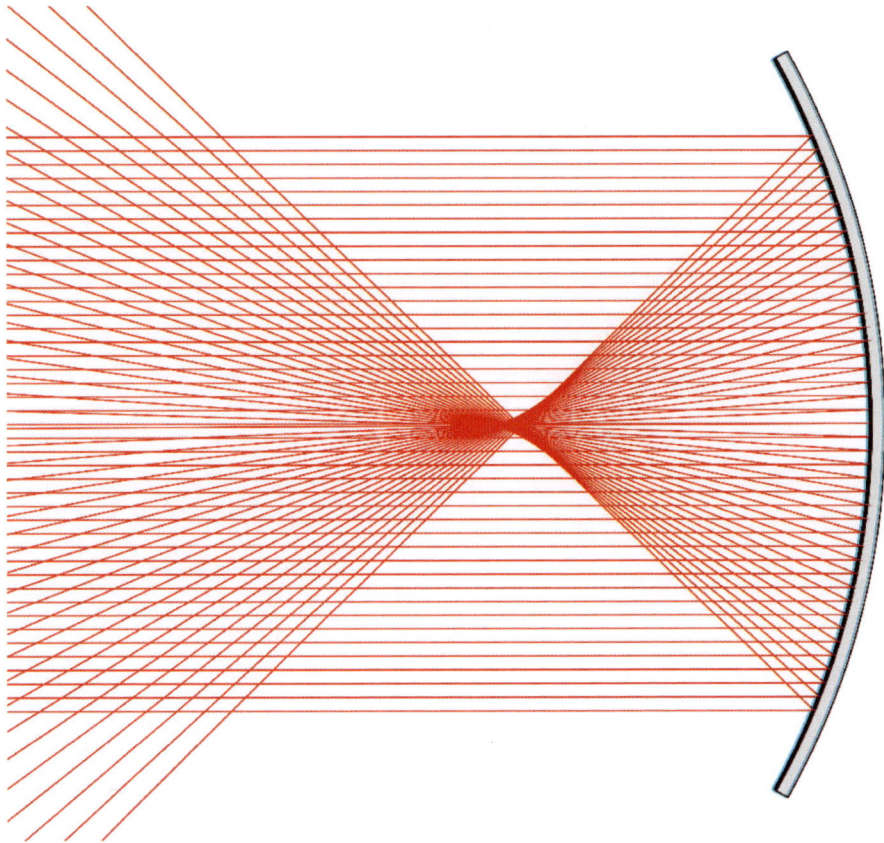

The next diagram shows parallel rays of light incident on a concave **parabolic** mirror. To the human eye, these two curved mirrors might not look very different, but mathematically they are, and a parabolic mirror has the shape of a **parabola**.

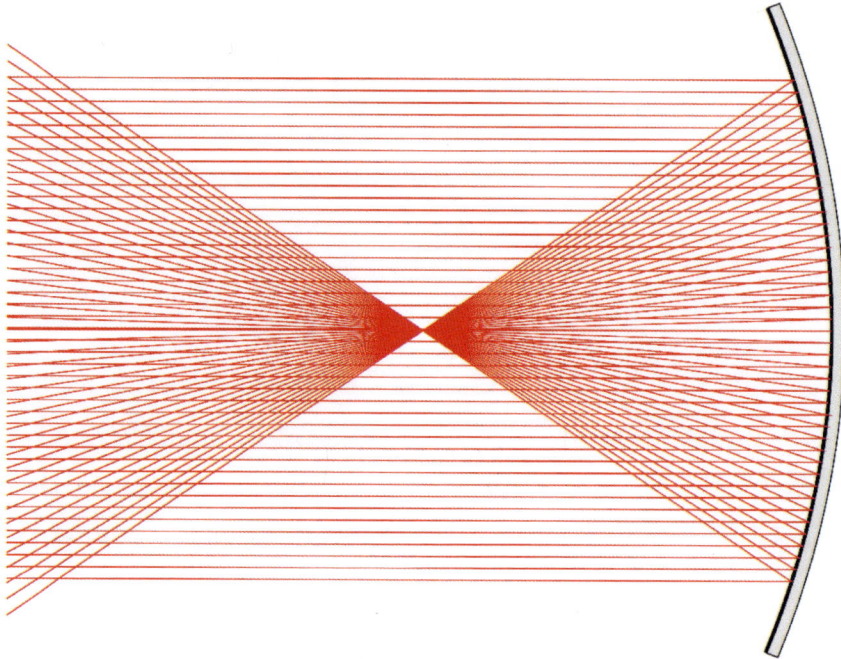

Describe the differences in the way the two types of mirror affect parallel light rays.

_____

_____

_____

_____

_____

[4 marks]

99.) The diagram below shows a cross-section of the design of a simple telescope. What type of telescope does it show?

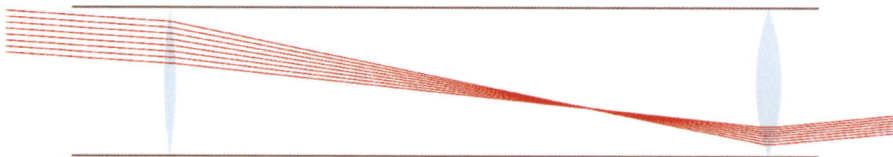

i.) a Galilean refracting telescope

ii.) a Cassegrain reflecting telescope

iii.) a Keplerian refracting telescope

iv.) a Newtonian reflecting telescope

[2 marks]

100.) The diagram below shows a cross-section of the design of a simple telescope. What type of telescope does it show?

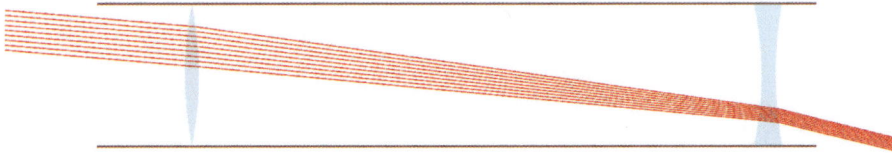

i.) a Galilean refracting telescope

ii.) a Newtonian reflecting telescope

iii.) a Cassegrain reflecting telescope

iv.) a Keplerian refracting telescope

[2 marks]

101.) The diagram below shows a cross-section of the design of a simple telescope. What type of telescope does it show?

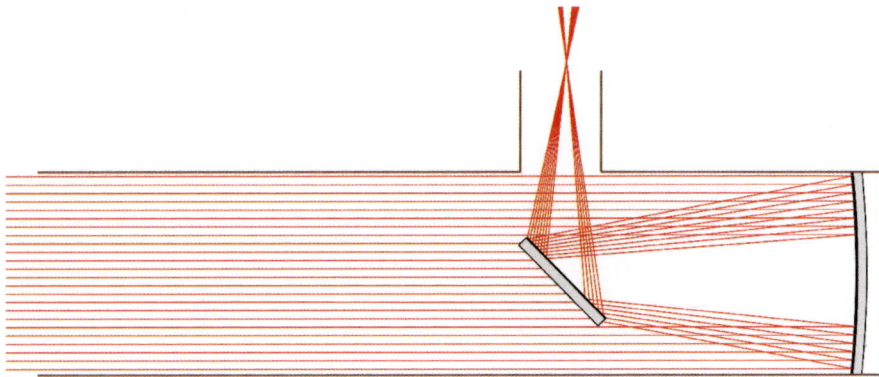

i.) a Newtonian reflecting telescope

ii.) a Cassegrain reflecting telescope

iii.) a Keplerian refracting telescope

iv.) a Galilean refracting telescope

[2 marks]

102.) The diagram below shows a cross-section of the design of a simple telescope. What type of telescope does it show?

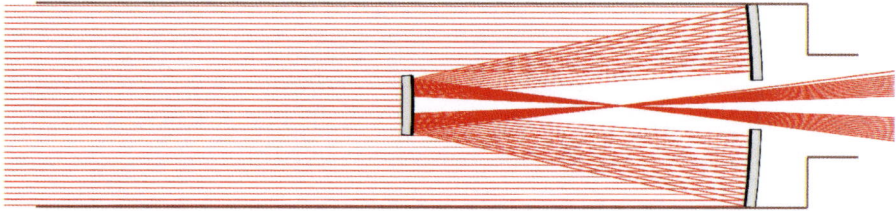

i.) a Keplerian refracting telescope

ii.) a Newtonian reflecting telescope

iii.) a Cassegrain reflecting telescope

iv.) a Galilean refracting telescope

[2 marks]

103.) The diagram below shows a cross-section of a Galilean refracting telescope. Label the objective lens and the eyepiece on the diagram.

[2 marks]

104.) Which of the following formulae relates the magnification produced by a telescope, m, to the focal length of its objective lens, f_o, and the focal length of its eyepiece, f_e?

i.) $m = f_o - f_e$

ii.) $m = f_o f_e$

iii.) $m = \frac{f_o}{f_e}$

iv.) $m = \frac{f_o^2}{f_e^2}$

[1 mark]

105.) A refracting telescope has an objective lens with a focal length of $40.25\,\text{cm}$, and an eyepiece with a focal length of $2.3\,\text{cm}$. What magnification does the telescope produce?

[2 marks]

106.) A refracting telescope has an objective lens with a focal length of $742.5\,\text{mm}$, and an eyepiece with a focal length of $45\,\text{mm}$. What magnification does the telescope produce?

_____

[2 marks]

107.) The diagram below shows a cross-section of a refracting telescope. Parallel rays of light are shown passing into the telescope from the left. The dashed line shows where the rays are focused.

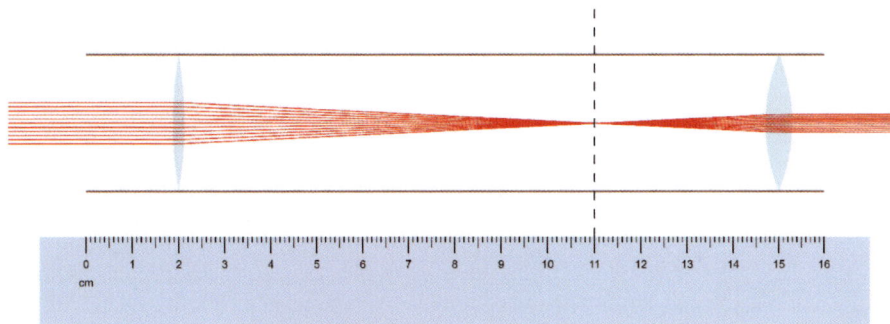

a.) What is the focal length of the objective lens?

_____

[2 marks]

b.) What is the focal length of the eyepiece?

_____

[2 marks]

c.) What magnification does this telescope produce?

_____

[2 marks]

108.) A refracting telescope is designed to have an eyepiece with a focal length of $3.8\,\text{cm}$. What focal length must the objective lens have for the telescope to produce a magnification of 17.0?

_____

[2 marks]

109.) A refracting telescope is designed to have an eyepiece with a focal length of 49 mm. What focal length must the objective lens have for the telescope to produce a magnification of 12.5?

_____

[2 marks]

110.) Complete the following sentence with one of the words given below.

The _____ the diameter of the objective element of a telescope, the greater its resolution.

   i.) greater   ii.) lesser

[1 mark]

111.) Complete the following sentence with one of the words given below.

The longer the wavelength of radiation a telescope is designed to observe, the _____ the diameter the objective element must have to achieve a given resolution.

   i.) greater   ii.) lesser

[1 mark]

112.) What is **chromatic aberration**?

_____

_____

_____

[4 marks]

113.) What is a **reflecting telescope**?

_____

_____

[2 marks]

114.) Explain why the largest telescopes in the world are reflecting telescopes, rather than refracting telescopes.

_____

_____

_____

[2 marks]

115.) No human missions have ever been sent to Mars, but several robotic vehicles have been sent to and landed on the planet. Describe the advantages and disadvantages of robotic missions to Mars compared to human missions.

_____

_____

_____

_____

_____

_____

_____

_____

_____

_____

_____

_____

_____

[8 marks]

116.) Below is a photograph of Venus, taken by the MESSENGER spacecraft in 2007.

Credit: NASA / Johns Hopkins University Applied Physics Laboratory / Carnegie Institution of Washington [8]

a.) Compare the **size** of Venus to the other inner planets of the solar system.

_____

_____

_____

[3 marks]

b.) Compare the **surface gravity** of Venus to Earth and Mars.

_____

_____

_____

[3 marks]

c.) Describe the **composition** of Venus' atmosphere.

_____

_____

_____

_____

_____

[4 marks]

d.) Describe the **temperature** and **pressure** conditions on Venus' surface, making note of how the atmosphere's chemical composition and size produces these conditions.

_____

_____

_____

_____

_____

_____

_____

[5 marks]

e.) Comment on whether humans could establish a base on the surface of Venus.

_____

_____

_____

_____

_____

[4 marks]

117.) Below is a photograph of Mercury, taken by the MESSENGER spacecraft in 2008.

Credit: NASA / Johns Hopkins University Applied Physics Laboratory / Arizona State University / Carnegie Institution of Washington [9]

a.) Compare the **size** of Mercury to the other planets of the solar system.

_____

_____

[**2 marks**]

b.) Describe the **atmosphere** of Mercury.

_____

[**2 marks**]

c.) Describe the **temperature** on Mercury's surface.

_____

_____

_____

_____

_____

_____

_____

[5 marks]

118.) Below is a photograph of Mars, taken by the Viking 1 orbiter in 1976.

Credit: NASA [10]

a.) Mars has a mean radius of 3390 km. Calculate the ratio of the mean radius of Mars to the mean radius of Earth. Use a value of $6370\,\mathrm{km}$ for the mean radius of Earth, and give your answer to 3 significant figures.

_____

[2 marks]

b.) Mars has a mean surface gravity of $3.72\,\frac{\mathrm{m}}{\mathrm{s}}$. Calculate the ratio of the mean surface gravity of Mars to the mean surface gravity of Earth. Use a value of $9.81\,\frac{\mathrm{m}}{\mathrm{s}}$ for the mean surface gravity of Earth, and give your answer to 3 significant figures.

_____

[2 marks]

c.) Describe the **composition** of Mars' atmosphere.

_____

_____

_____

[4 marks]

d.) Earth's atmosphere is about 80% nitrogen and 20% oxygen. If humans were to establish a base on Mars, they would need to breathe air similar in composition to this. Describe a possible source for this air on Mars.

_____

_____

_____

_____

_____

[3 marks]

119.) Why is liquid water considered to be very important for life?

_____

_____

_____

_____

_____

[4 marks]

120.) Below is a photograph of Titan, one of Saturn's moons.

Credit: NASA / JPL-Caltech / SSI / Kevin M. Gill [11]

a.) Compare the **size** of Titan to the other moons and the planets and dwarf planets in the solar system.

_____

_____

_____

_____

_____

_____

_____

[5 marks]

b.) Compare the **atmosphere** of Titan to other moons in the solar system.

_____

_____

_____

[3 marks]

c.) Describe the **composition** and **basic structure** of Titan's atmosphere.

_____

_____

_____

_____

_____

[5 marks]

121.) Below is a photograph of Europa, one of Jupiter's moons.

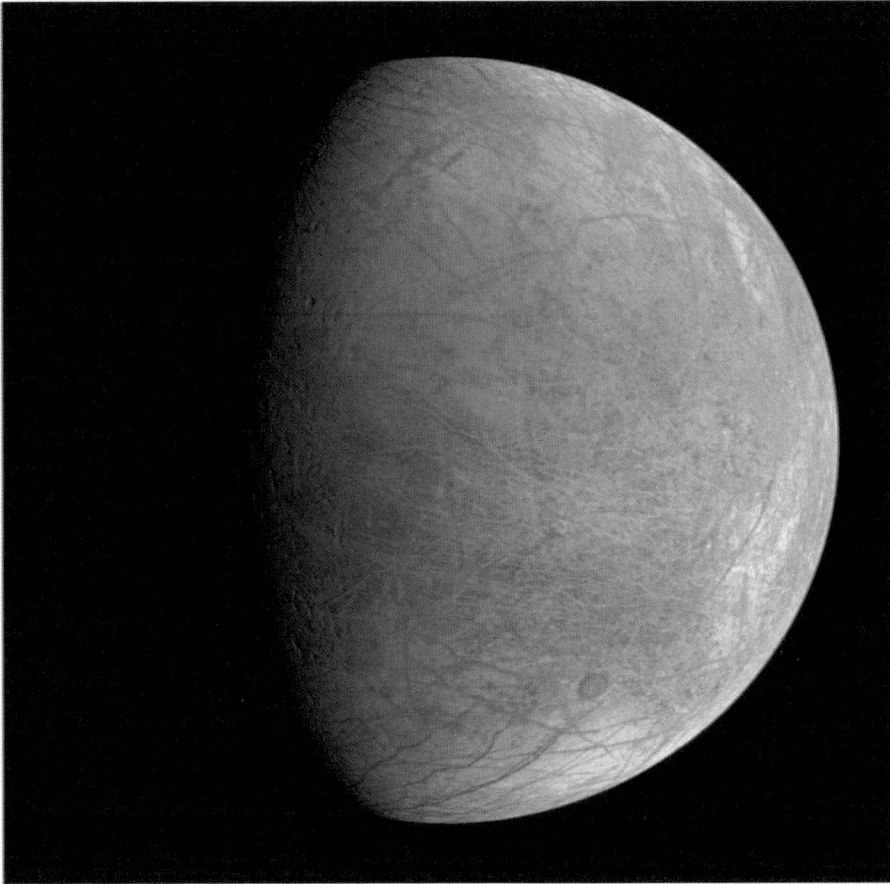

Credit: NASA / JPL-Caltech / SwRI / MSSS / Kevin M. Gill [12]

a.) Compare the **size** of Europa to the other moons of Jupiter, and the other moons in the solar system.

_____

_____

_____

[3 marks]

b.) Describe the **surface conditions** on Europa.

_____

_____

_____

_____

[5 marks]

c.) Europa is a candidate for finding extraterrestrial life. Where might life exist on Europa?

_____

_____

_____

_____

_____

_____

[4 marks]

122.) What is the **Drake Equation**?

_____

_____

_____

[2 marks]

123.) One of the factors in the Drake Equation is R_*, which represents the average rate of star formation in the galaxy. Explain why this is a factor in the Drake Equation.

_____

_____

_____

_____

[3 marks]

124.) The values produced by the Drake Equation for the likely number of planets with civilisations in the galaxy vary hugely – from about 20 to about 100,000,000. Why is this?

_____

_____

[2 marks]

125.) What is meant by the term 'the habitable zone around a star'?

_____

_____

[3 marks]

126.) Describe the **transit method** for finding exoplanets.

_____

_____

_____

_____

[3 marks]

127.) Describe the **astrometry method** for finding exoplanets.

_____

_____

_____

_____

_____

_____

[3 marks]

128.) Describe the **radial velocity method** for finding exoplanets.

_____

_____

_____

_____

_____

_____

_____

_____

_____

_____

[4 marks]

129.) Explain why it is very difficult to detect exoplanets directly using optical telescopes.

_____

_____

_____

_____

_____

_____

[4 marks]

130.) TRAPPIST-1 is a star about 41 light-years away from Earth. It is an ultra-cool red dwarf star with a mass about 9% of that of the Sun. TRAPPIST-1 has 7 known exoplanets in orbit around it, all of which are of comparable size to the inner planets of the solar system.

a.) Would the habitable zone around TRAPPIST-1 be **closer to** or **further away from** the star than the habitable zone of the solar system?

   i.) further away from the star

  ii.) closer to the star

[1 mark]

b.) All 7 known exoplanets of the TRAPPIST-1 system have orbital semi-major axes less than 0.07 AU. Compare the size of the TRAPPIST-1 system to the orbits of the planets in the solar system.

   i.) The planets of the TRAPPIST-1 system all orbit at smaller distances than Mercury does in the solar system.

[1 mark]

131.) Below is an artist's impression of the exoplanet TRAPPIST 1e. This exoplanet was discovered in 2017 by the Spitzer Space Telescope.

Credit: NASA / JPL-Caltech [13]

The table below gives some data about TRAPPIST 1e.

Property	Value
Mass	$0.772 M_{\text{Earth}}$
Mean Radius	$0.910 R_{\text{Earth}}$
Surface Gravity	$0.930g$
Surface Temperature	$246\,\text{K}$

Based on this data, is TRAPPIST 1e likely to be a habitable planet?

i.) Yes   ii.) No

[2 marks]

132.) Below is an artist's impression of the exoplanet TRAPPIST 1f. This exoplanet was discovered in 2017 by the Spitzer Space Telescope.

Credit: NASA / JPL-Caltech [14]

The table below gives some data about TRAPPIST 1f.

Property	Value
Mass	$0.68 M_{\text{Earth}}$
Mean Radius	$1.05 R_{\text{Earth}}$
Surface Gravity	$0.62g$
Surface Temperature	$219\,\text{K}$

Based on this data, is TRAPPIST 1e likely to be a habitable planet?

i.) Yes   ii.) No

[2 marks]

133.) Below is an artist's impression of the exoplanet Proxima Centauri d. Proxima Centauri d is the **closest exoplanet to Earth**.

Credit: ESO / L. Calçada [15]

The table below gives some data about the exoplanet.

Property	Value
Mass	$0.26 M_{\text{Earth}}$
Mean Radius	$0.81 R_{\text{Earth}}$
Surface Temperature	$360\,\text{K}$

a.) Based on this data, is Proxima Centauri d likely to be a habitable planet?

i.) Yes   ii.) No

[2 marks]

b.) The Proxima Centauri system is 4.2 light-years away from Earth. If we could build a spacecraft that could travel at 0.25 times the speed of light, how long would it take us to reach Proxima Centauri d? Use a value of $3 \times 10^8\,\frac{\text{m}}{\text{s}}$ for the speed of light, and give your answer in years to 1 decimal place.

_____

[3 marks]

134.) Gliese 876c is an exoplanet orbiting the red dwarf star Gliese 876. The planet was discovered in 2001. The table below gives some data about Gliese 876c.

Property	Value
Mass	$266 M_{\text{Earth}}$
Orbital Period	$30.1\,\text{days}$
Orbital Eccentricity	0.257

Based on this data, is Gliese 876c likely to be a habitable, rocky planet?

  i.) Yes   ii.) No

[2 marks]

135.) What quantity is a **light-year** a unit of?

  i.) speed   ii.) length   iii.) time

[1 mark]

136.) Give the definition of a **light-year**.

_____

_____

_____

[2 marks]

137.) What is the unit symbol for **light-years**?

  i.) yr   ii.) ly   iii.) Ly   iv.) LY

[1 mark]

138.) What is $1\,\text{ly}$ in metres?

  i.) $1.5 \times 10^{11}\,\text{m}$ ii.) $9.46 \times 10^{15}\,\text{m}$ iii.) $3.09 \times 10^{16}\,\text{m}$ iv.) $9.46 \times 10^{16}\,\text{m}$

[1 mark]

139.) What is the unit symbol for **kilo-light-years**?

  i.) kly   ii.) kLY   iii.) Kly   iv.) klyr

[1 mark]

140.) How many light-years are there in one kilo-light-year?

i.) 1000000   ii.) 1000   iii.) 100   iv.) 1000000000

[1 mark]

141.) What is the unit symbol for **mega-light-years**?

i.) Mly   ii.) MLY   iii.) mLy   iv.) Mlyr

[1 mark]

142.) How many light-years are there in one mega-light-year?

i.) 10000000   ii.) 1000000   iii.) 100   iv.) 1000000000

[1 mark]

143.) What is $65.8\,ly$ in metres? Give your answer to 3 significant figures.

_____

[2 marks]

144.) What is $5.8 \times 10^{17}\,m$ in light-years? Give your answer to 3 significant figures.

_____

[2 marks]

145.) What is $8.5\,ly$ in kilometres? Give your answer to 3 significant figures.

_____

[2 marks]

146.) What is $7.46 \times 10^{14}\,km$ in light-years? Give your answer to 3 significant figures.

_____

[2 marks]

147.) What is $68.7\,kly$ in metres? Give your answer to 3 significant figures.

_____

[2 marks]

148.) What is $9.46 \times 10^{19}\,m$ in kilo-light-years? Give your answer to 3 significant figures.

_____

[**2 marks**]

149.) Give the definition of a **light-second**.

_____

_____

_____

[**2 marks**]

150.) How many metres are there in 1 light-second? Give an exact answer.

_____

[**2 marks**]

ANSWERS

1.) the Sun

2.) the Earth

3.) It showed that objects could orbit things *other than* the Earth. In the geocentric model, everything orbits the Earth. The moons of Jupiter showed that not everything had to orbit the Earth.

4.) The parallax effect is too small to observe without a telescope, because the stars are an extremely long way away.

5.) retrograde motion

6.) The shape of a planet's orbit is an ellipse with the Sun at one focus.

7.)

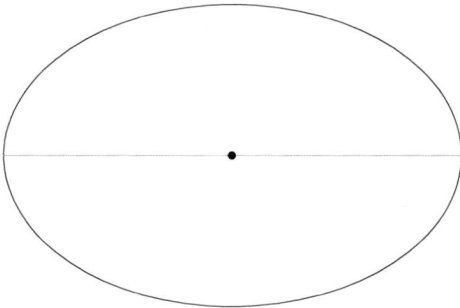

8.)

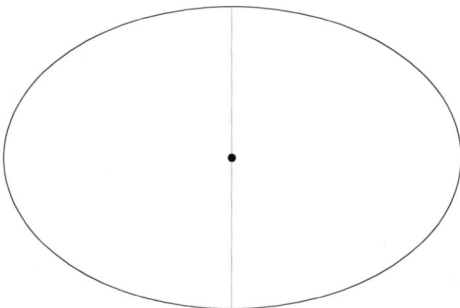

9.)

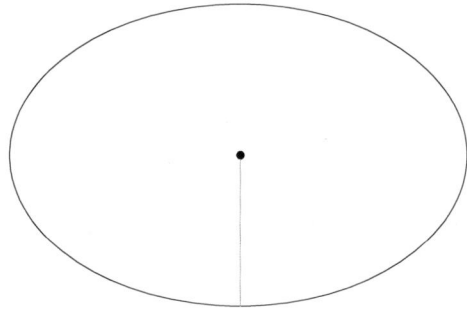

10.)

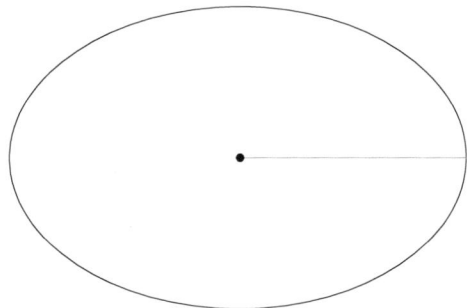

11.)

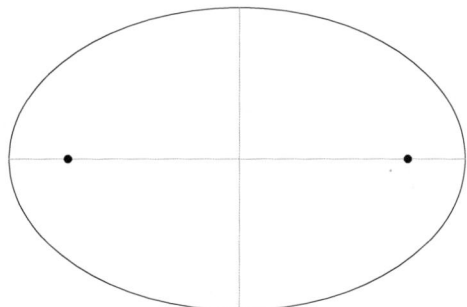

12.)

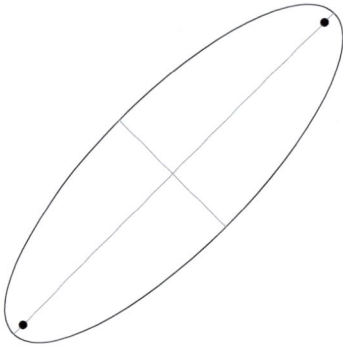

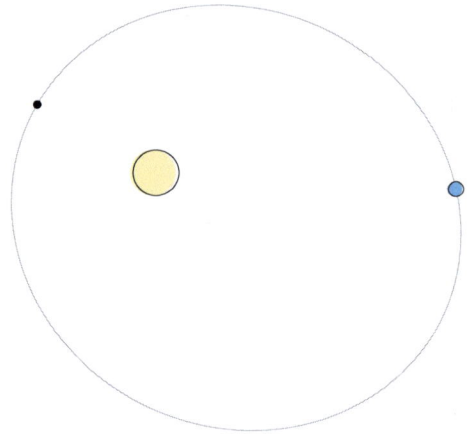

13.) a.) D

13.) b.) C

14.) a.) B

14.) b.) D

15.) A circle is a special case of an ellipse where the semi-major axis and semi-minor axis are equal, and are just called the 'radius' of the circle.

16.)

18.)

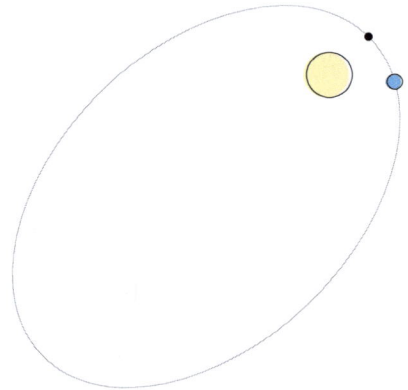

19.)

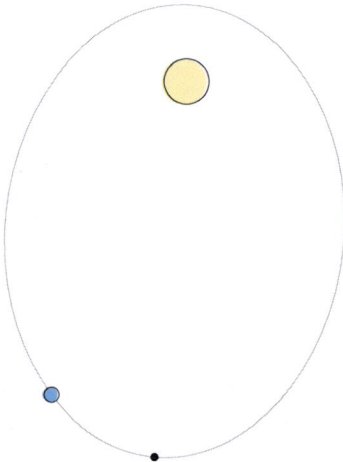

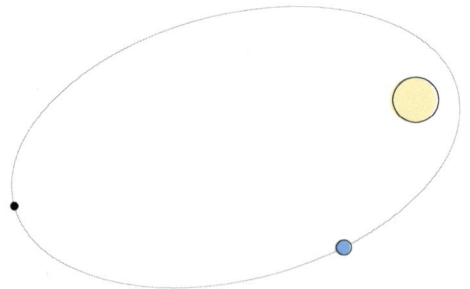

20.) For an object that orbits the Sun, its perihelion is the point in its orbit when it is closest to the Sun.

21.) For an object that orbits the Sun, its aphelion is the point in its orbit when it is furthest away from the Sun.

17.)

22.)

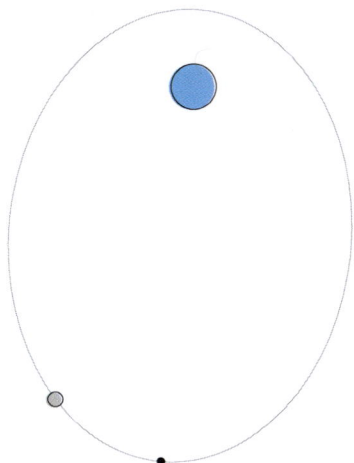

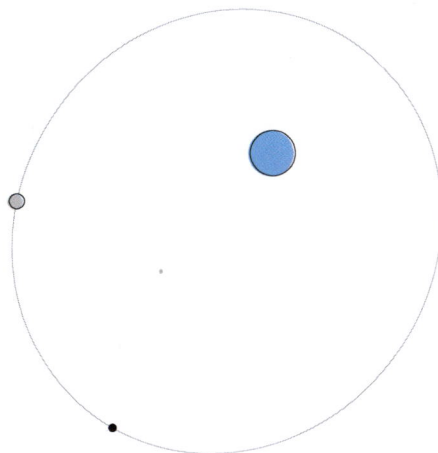

23.)

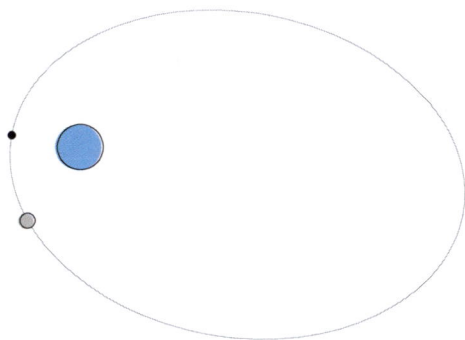

26.) For an object that orbits the Earth, its apogee is the point in its orbit when it is furthest away from the Earth.

27.) For an object that orbits the Earth, its perigee is the point in its orbit when it is closest to the Earth.

28.)

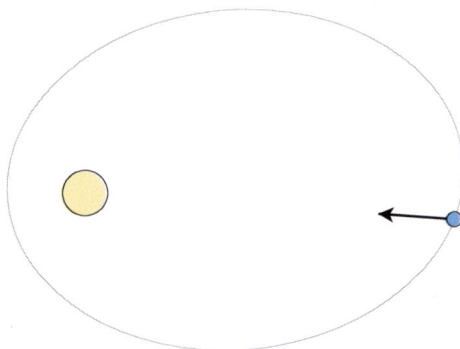

24.)

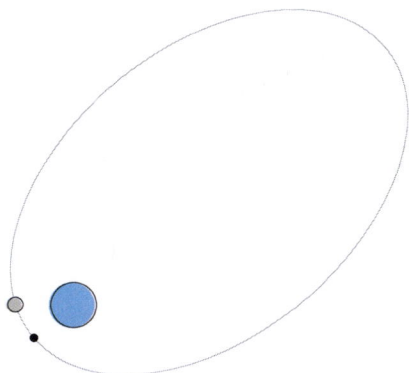

29.)

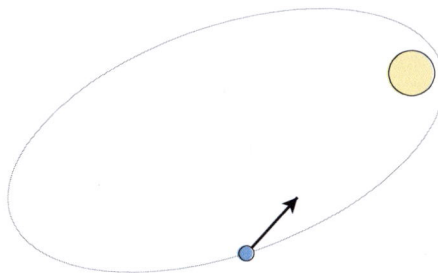

25.)

30.)

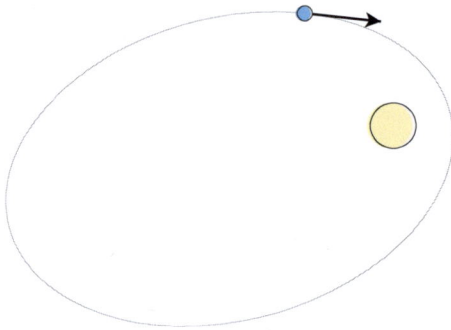

31.)

32.) The imaginary line connecting the Earth to the Sun sweeps out equal areas in equal times as the Earth moves along its orbit.

33.) $\frac{T^2}{a^3} = $ constant

34.) $\frac{T_1^2}{a_1^3} = \frac{T_2^2}{a_2^3}$

35.) the mass of the host star

36.) $5.2\,\mathrm{AU}$

37.) $19.2\,\mathrm{AU}$

38.) $2040\,\mathrm{y}$

39.) The gravitational force between two objects is **proportional** to the **product** of the masses of the two objects.

40.) The gravitational force between two objects is **inversely proportional** to the distance between the centres of mass of the objects **squared**.

41.) Mars

42.) Jupiter

43.) Venus

44.) Mercury

45.) Uranus

46.) 2

47.) 4

48.) 5

49.) 2

50.) Mercury

51.) Neptune

52.) Venus

53.) Mercury

54.) Neptune

55.) Jupiter

56.) Venus

57.) Mercury

58.) Neptune

59.) Mars

60.) anticlockwise

61.) B

62.) 22.8

63.) The ecliptic is the orbital plane of the Earth around the Sun. Most of the planets, dwarf planets, and asteroids in the solar system orbit in or close to the ecliptic.

64.) a.) Mercurial, Mercurian

64.) b.) Venusian, Venerean, Venerian, Cytherean

64.) c.) Terrestrial, Terran, Tellurian

64.) d.) Martian

64.) e.) Jovian

64.) f.) Saturnian, Cronian, Kronian

64.) g.) Uranian

64.) h.) Neptunian, Poseidean

65.) a.) a gas giant

65.) b.) Jupiter is the largest planet in the solar system. It is much larger than the inner planets.

65.) c.) hydrogen

65.) d.) $1330 \frac{\text{kg}}{\text{m}^3}$

65.) e.) The average density of Jupiter is **less than** the average density of Earth.

66.) The rings of Saturn are mostly made of small particles of water ice.

67.) The asteroid belt is a torus-shaped region between Mars and Jupiter that contains a large number of asteroids.

68.) The Kuiper Belt is a region beyond the orbit of Neptune that contains many small objects made of rock, metal, and ice. The Kuiper Belt also contains many dwarf planets, including Pluto, Makemake, and Haumea.

69.) The Oort Cloud is a hypothetical region approximately 2000 to 200000 AU away from the Sun containing a large number of asteroids and comets. It is thought to be the origin of many long-period comets.

70.) The heliosphere is the region of space dominated by solar wind. It extends far out beyond the orbit of Pluto.

71.) The heliopause is the boundary between the heliosphere and interstellar space.

72.) Ceres is located in the asteroid belt between Mars and Jupiter.

73.) Makemake is located beyond the orbit of Neptune in the Kuiper Belt.

74.) Pluto is not considered to be a planet because it has not cleared the region of its orbit of other large masses. Pluto accounts for only a small proportion of the total mass in its orbit.

75.) a comet

76.) Comets typically have orbits with **high eccentricities**.

77.) Comet nuclei are composed of rock and various 'ices', such as water ice and frozen carbon dioxide, carbon monoxide, methane, and ammonia.

78.) It is a very thin atmosphere around the comet formed from gas and dust ejected from the comet's nucleus.

79.) The ion tail points directly away from the Sun in a straight line, as the ions are more strongly affected by the solar wind than the dust. The dust tail forms a curved line.

80.) It is a mixture of small particles of minerals, such as olivine, pyroxenes, and other silicates, as well as trace quantities of heavy metals.

81.) a short period comet

82.) a short period comet

83.) the asteroid belt

84.) Asteroids have a wide range of compositions. They are usually a mix of metals, such as nickel and iron, rock minerals, such as olivine and pyroxenes, and some ices, such as water ice, carbon dioxide ice, and ammonia ice.

85.) Meteors are pieces of rock and ice from space that enter Earth's atmosphere.

86.) A meteorite is a meteor that reaches the ground.

87.) Meteoroids are small pieces of rock and metal in space. They are significantly smaller than asteroids, ranging from a few millimetres to up to about a metre wide.

88.) A refracting telescope is a telescope that uses lenses to magnify the image of an object.

89.) a convex lens

90.) a concave lens

91.) converging

92.) diverging

93.) a convex ideal lens

94.) a concave ideal lens

95.) With the ideal convex lens, the parallel light rays are modelled as being focused to a single point. However, with a real convex lens, parallel light rays are not focused exactly to a single point, but to a region. Real convex lenses do not focus light perfectly.

96.) a concave mirror

97.) a convex mirror

98.) A spherical concave mirror does not focus light perfectly to a single point. A parabolic concave mirror *does* focus light perfectly to a single point.

99.) a Keplerian refracting telescope

100.) a Galilean refracting telescope

101.) a Newtonian reflecting telescope

102.) a Cassegrain reflecting telescope

103.)

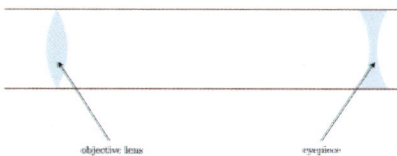

objective lens   eyepiece

104.) $m = \frac{f_o}{f_e}$

105.) 17.5

106.) 16.5

107.) a.) $9\,\text{cm}$

107.) b.) $4\,\text{cm}$

107.) c.) 2.25

108.) $64.6\,\text{cm}$

109.) $612.5\,\text{mm}$

110.) greater

111.) greater

112.) Chromatic aberration is an imperfect focusing of light rays of different colours, due to the refractive index of a lens material being different at different wavelengths.

113.) A reflecting telescope is a telescope that uses curved mirrors to magnify the image of an object.

114.) Manufacturing large lenses of exactly the right shape is much harder than manufacturing large mirrors of exactly the right shape.

115.) It takes many months to get to Mars from Earth. Astronauts sent to Mars would have to take many months' worth of food with them. This is not necessary for robotic missions. Robot missions require no life support systems to recycle air and water either, so the craft lifted into space by rocket can be much lighter. Humans who went to Mars would also have to be brought back, whereas robotic vehicles can be left there, drastically reducing the amount of fuel needed. Astronauts sent to Mars would have to endure many months of low gravity, which can negatively affect the human body. They would also be exposed to high energy radiation from space, which is largely blocked by Earth's atmosphere and magnetosphere. Robotic craft are largely unaffected by low gravity and the high-energy radiation of space. Robotic vehicles are limited by the tools and machinery they take with them, whereas humans can adapt to the environment around them very easily.

116.) a.) Venus is the second-largest of the inner planets. It's much larger than Mercury and Mars, but only slightly smaller than Earth.

116.) b.) Venus' surface gravity is very similar to that of Earth, at about 90% of Earth's gravity. Both Venus and Earth have much stronger gravity than Mars.

116.) c.) Venus' atmosphere is mostly carbon dioxide (97%). It contains a much higher proportion of sulfur dioxide than Earth's atmosphere does, leading to the presence of sulfuric acid in the atmosphere.

116.) d.) The mass of Venus' atmosphere is much greater than that of Earth – about 92 times greater. This means that the pressure at the surface is much greater than the pressure on the surface of Earth – again about 92 times greater. As carbon dioxide produces a strong greenhouse effect, the temperature at Venus' surface is extremely high – hotter than the surface of Mercury – at $464\,°\text{C}$.

116.) e.) Humans could not establish a base on the surface of Venus. The pressure would crush most structures, and the acid in the atmosphere would erode many of the substances the structure was built out of.

117.) a.) Mercury is the smallest planet in the solar system.

117.) b.) Mercury has effectively no atmosphere.

117.) c.) The temperature on Mercury's surface varies greatly, from about $-200\,°C$ to several hundred degrees Celsius. This is because Mercury is very close to the Sun, so is heated by it, but has no atmosphere to contain and circulate the heat.

118.) a.) 0.532

118.) b.) 0.379

118.) c.) Mars' atmosphere is mostly carbon dioxide (96%). It is about 2% argon and 2% nitrogen, and has small amounts of oxygen, carbon monoxide, and water vapour.

118.) d.) The oxygen humans need to breathe could be produced on Mars by electrolysing water from Mars' polar ice caps, which would produce hydrogen and oxygen. Nitrogen could be refined from Mars' atmosphere.

119.) Lots of chemicals can dissolve in liquid water, and when they are dissolved in water the molecules can move around easily and react with each other. Water allows chemicals to undergo the complex reactions involved in life.

120.) a.) Titan is the second-largest moon in the solar system. The only moon larger than Titan is Jupiter's moon Ganymede. Titan is larger than Earth's moon, with a radius about 1.5 times that of the Moon. Titan is larger than the planet Mercury. It is also larger than all of the dwarf planets, such as Pluto.

120.) b.) Titan is the only moon known to have a dense atmosphere. The other moons of the solar system either have no atmosphere or a very thin atmosphere.

120.) c.) Titan's atmosphere is mostly nitrogen (94.2%), with some methane and hydrogen. It has very little oxygen. The atmospheric pressure on the surface of Titan is about 1.5 times that on the surface of Earth.

121.) a.) Europa is the smallest of the four Galilean moons of Jupiter, but it is the sixth largest moon in the solar system.

121.) b.) Europa has an extremely thin atmosphere, so the pressure on its surface is very low, and the temperature is very low. This low pressure and temperature means that no liquid exists on the surface of Europa.

121.) c.) Life is very unlikely to exist on Europa's surface. However, it's thought that Europa has a subsurface saltwater ocean, as a result of tidal interactions with Jupiter. As water is essential for life on Earth, it's thought that life could develop in other large bodies of water in the solar system, such as Europa's subsurface ocean.

122.) The Drake Equation is an equation for estimating the probability of finding intelligent, extraterrestrial life.

123.) Life can only develop on planets and moons, and planets and moons only form around stars, so the more stars that form, the more planets and moons that form, and the more life that develops.

124.) The parameters of the equation are extremely hard to estimate.

125.) It is the range of orbits around the star within which liquid water could exist on a planet's surface.

126.) If a planet's orbit takes it between its host star and the Earth, some of the light from the star will be blocked from reaching Earth while the planet is in front of it. This can be detected by taking repeated flux measurements of the star, even though the planet only blocks a small proportion of the light.

127.) The astrometry method involves taking very precise measurements of the position of a star in the night sky. Any planets that are orbiting the star will make the star appear to 'wobble' due to their gravitational influence. From this 'wobble', some of the properties of the orbiting planets can be determined.

128.) A star that has a planet in orbit around it will move back and forth slightly due to the gravitational pull of the planet, as long as the view of the star system from Earth does not look directly down onto it. The motion towards and further away from Earth can be measured by looking at the shift in the absorption lines in the spectrum of light from the star. From this motion, some properties of the orbiting planet can be determined.

129.) Planets do not emit light; they only reflect light from the star they orbit. As they also have much smaller surface areas than stars, the amount of light received from them at Earth is very low. This makes them very difficult to detect optically.

130.) a.) closer to the star

130.) b.) The planets of the TRAPPIST-1 system all orbit at smaller distances than Mercury does in the solar system.

131.) Yes

132.) Yes

133.) a.) Yes

133.) b.) $16.8\,\mathrm{y}$

134.) No

135.) length

136.) One light-year is the distance that a beam of light will travel in free space in one year if it is not obstructed.

137.) ly

138.) $9.46 \times 10^{15}\,\mathrm{m}$

139.) kly

140.) 1000

141.) Mly

142.) 1000000

143.) $6.23 \times 10^{17}\,\mathrm{m}$

144.) $61.3\,\mathrm{ly}$

145.) $8.04 \times 10^{13}\,\mathrm{km}$

146.) $78.9\,\mathrm{ly}$

147.) $6.5 \times 10^{20}\,\mathrm{m}$

148.) $10\,\mathrm{kly}$

149.) One light-second is the distance that a beam of light will travel in free space in one second if it is not obstructed.

150.) $299792458\,\mathrm{m}$

IMAGES USED

[1] **A photograph of Jupiter, taken by the Hubble Space Telescope in 2014**
NASA, ESA, and A. Simon (Goddard Space Flight Center)
Public Domain
https://commons.wikimedia.org/wiki/File:Jupiter_and_its_shrunken_Great_Red_Spot.jpg

[2] **A photograph of Saturn at a high exposure to show the rings clearly, taken by Cassini in 2007**
NASA
Public Domain
https://commons.wikimedia.org/wiki/File:Saturn_from_Cassini_Orbiter_(2007-01-19).jpg

[3] **A true-colour image of the dwarf planet Ceres, taken by the Dawn spacecraft in 2015**
NASA / JPL-Caltech / UCLA / MPS / DLR / IDA / Justin Cowart
Public Domain
https://commons.wikimedia.org/wiki/File:Ceres_-_RC3_-_Haulani_Crater_(22381131691)_(cropped).jpg

[4] **An image of the dwarf planet Makemake, taken by the Hubble Space Telescope in 2015**
NASA, ESA, and A. Parker and M. Buie (Southwest Research Institute)
Creative Commons Attribution 4.0 International
https://commons.wikimedia.org/wiki/File:Makemake_and_its_moon.jpg

[5] **A true-colour image of Pluto, taken by the New Horizons spacecraft in 2015**
NASA / Johns Hopkins University Applied Physics Laboratory / Southwest Research Institute / Alex Parker
Public Domain
https://commons.wikimedia.org/wiki/File:Pluto_in_True_Color_-_High-Res.jpg

[6] **A photograph of Comet Lovejoy, taken by NASA astronaut Dan Burbank from the International Space Station in 2011**
NASA / Dan Burbank
Public Domain
https://en.wikipedia.org/wiki/File:Iss030e015472_Edit.jpg

[7] **A photograph of the asteroid Vesta, taken by the Dawn spacecraft in 2011**
NASA / JPL / MPS / DLR / IDA / Björn Jónsson

Public Domain

`https://commons.wikimedia.org/wiki/File:Vesta_in_natural_color.jpg`

[8] **A photograph of Venus, taken by the MESSENGER spacecraft in 2007**
NASA / Johns Hopkins University Applied Physics Laboratory / Carnegie Institution of Washington
Public Domain

`https://commons.wikimedia.org/wiki/File:Venus_2_Approach_Image.jpg`

[9] **A true-colour image of Mercury, taken by the MESSENGER spacecraft in 2008**
NASA / Johns Hopkins University Applied Physics Laboratory / Arizona State University / Carnegie Institution of Washington
Public Domain

`https://commons.wikimedia.org/wiki/File:Mercury_in_true_color.jpg`

[10] **A photograph of Mars, taken by the Viking 1 orbiter in 1976**
NASA
Public Domain

`https://commons.wikimedia.org/wiki/File:Mars_atmosphere.jpg`

[11] **A photograph of Saturn's moon Titan, taken by Cassini in 2011**
NASA / JPL-Caltech / SSI / Kevin M. Gill
Creative Commons Attribution 2.0 Generic

`https://commons.wikimedia.org/wiki/File:Titan_in_true_color_by_Kevin_M._Gill.jpg`

[12] **A photograph of Jupiter's moon Europa, taken by the Juno spacecraft**
NASA / JPL-Caltech / SwRI / MSSS / Kevin M. Gill
Creative Commons Attribution 3.0 Unported

`https://commons.wikimedia.org/wiki/File:Europa_in_natural_color.png`

[13] **An artist's impression of the exoplanet TRAPPIST 1e**
NASA / JPL-Caltech
Public Domain

`https://commons.wikimedia.org/wiki/File:TRAPPIST-1e_artist_impression_2018.png`

[14] **An artist's impression of the exoplanet TRAPPIST 1f**
NASA / JPL-Caltech
Public Domain

`https://commons.wikimedia.org/wiki/File:TRAPPIST-1f_artist_impression_2018.png`

[15] **An artist's impression of the exoplanet Proxima Centauri d**
ESO / L. Calçada
Creative Commons Attribution 4.0 International

`https://www.eso.org/public/images/eso2202a/`

DID YOU LIKE THIS BOOK?

If you liked this book, consider giving it a review where you bought it. This will help others to find the book.

Printed in Great Britain
by Amazon